A STUNNING SUCCESS

A round of Christmas gaieties was climaxed on the evening of January 31, 1771, with a wedding for Mary Wheatley and John Lathrop in the big house on King Street.

After the ceremony, when the cake had been cut, Mrs. Wheatley lifted her hand and said, "Our Phillis has written a poem for this happy occasion. Now if you please, ladies and gentlemen, she will recite it for you."

There was a light patter of hands and much craning of necks as the dark girl came from her place behind the serving table and stood beside her mistress. She looked around a moment and then began to speak....

The guests were delighted and Phillis' sweet, musical voice and deep set eyes held them entranced. For nearly twenty minutes Phillis declaimed her lines. She bowed amid enthusiastic applause. "How sweet!" "She's a genius!" "A black poetess!"

THE STORY OF PHILLIS WHEATLEY
was originally published by
Julian Messner.

Critics' Corner:

"Sympathetic and revealing portrait of the gentle, devout, and freedom-loving Afro-American poet of Revolutionary War days. Rescued as a small child from the slave market and taken into their home and educated by the John Wheatleys of Boston, Phillis began writing poetry at an early age, winning recognition both in Boston and in England from such people as George Washington and the Countess of Huntingdon."
—A.L.A. Booklist

"...it merits high praise for its interpretation of a period and person."
—Saturday Review

"Her triumphs and her sorrows make a moving tale...."
—The New York Times

"Miss Graham has written another of her fine biographies for young people."
—Catholic School Journal

Other Recommendations: Child Study Association; Bro-Dart Foundation, Elementary School Library Collection; Horn Book; Library Journal (especially recommended); H. S. Wilson Junior High School Library Catalog; National Council of Teachers of English.

About the Author:

SHIRLEY GRAHAM studied at the Sorbonne in Paris and at Oberlin College in Ohio where she took her master's degree. In 1938 she was awarded a Julius Rosenwald Fellowship for Creative Writing, and in 1947 she received a Guggenheim Fellowship. Another of her popular biographies for young people, *Dr. George Washington Carver: Scientist,* is also an Archway Paperback.

THE
STORY OF
PHILLIS WHEATLEY

Phillis Wheatley

(FROM AN OLD STEEL ENGRAVING)

THE STORY OF PHILLIS WHEATLEY

by Shirley Graham

Illustrated by Robert Burns

AN ARCHWAY PAPERBACK
POCKET BOOKS • NEW YORK

THE STORY OF PHILLIS WHEATLEY

Julian Messner edition published 1949

Archway Paperback edition published June, 1969
4th printing .... September, 1975

L

Published by
POCKET BOOKS, a division of Simon & Schuster, Inc.,
630 Fifth Avenue, New York, N.Y.

Archway Paperback editions are distributed in the
U.S. by Simon & Schuster, Inc., 630 Fifth Avenue,
New York, N.Y. 10020, and in Canada by Simon &
Schuster of Canada, Ltd., Markham, Ontario, Canada.

Standard Book Number: 671-29762-7.
This Archway Paperback edition is published by arrange-
ment with Julian Messner. Copyright, 1949, by Shirley
Graham. All rights reserved. This book, or portions thereof,
may not be reproduced by any means without permission
of the original publisher: Julian Messner, a division of
Simon & Schuster, Inc., 1 West 39th Street,
New York, New York 10018.
Printed in the U.S.A.

Contents

INTRODUCTION

Should you, my lords, while you peruse my song,
Wonder from whence my love of Freedom sprung,
Whence flow these wishes for the common good,
By feeling hearts alone best understood,
I, young in life, by seeming cruel fate
Was snatched from Afric's distant happy seat;
Steeled was that soul and by no misery moved
That from a mother seized her babe beloved:
Such was my case. And can I then but pray
Others may never feel tyrannic sway?

Phillis Wheatley's first poem was published in 1770, five years before the beginning of the American Revolution and thirty years before the birth of German idealism. She wrote before that great pouring forth of the human spirit which gave the world Heine, Goethe and Schiller in Germany; Byron, Keats and Shelley in England; she died long before the flowering of New England. Her poetry was of the eighteenth century. Pope and Gray in England were the great poets of her day.

We offer no defense as to the merits of Phillis Wheatley's poems, but rest our case on the class of poetry of her day, on the comments of George Washington, on the reception her work was given in London and on the several editions of her poems after her death. However we may judge her poems by the absolute standards of literature, the fact remains that in her own day Phillis Wheatley was regarded as a young person of rare gifts.

It is the life of Phillis Wheatley which we would set down because she lived beautifully. It is this beauty we would capture for our own living.

Since making the study for this book I do not believe that Phillis Wheatley has been neglected primarily because she was a Negro. She was a casualty of war. She who sang so nobly of freedom was herself a victim of the war that freed thirteen separate colonies and founded a nation on the proposition that "All men are created equal."

AFFIDAVIT

Published in the first edition of Phillis Wheatley's poems,
London, 1773.

"We, whose names are underwritten, do assure the
World that the Poems specified in the following pages,
were (as we verily believe) written by Phillis, a
young Négro Girl, who was, but a few Years since,
bought, an uncultivated Barbarian, from Africa, and
has ever since been, and now is, under the disadvantage of serving as a slave in a Family in this Town. She
has been examined by some of the best Judges, and is
thought qualified to write them."
(Signed)

His Excellency, Thomas Hutchinson, Governor
The Hon. Andrew Oliver, Lieut. Governor.
The Hon. Thomas Hubbard,
The Hon. John Irving,
The Hon. James Pitts,
The Hon. Harrison Gray,
The Hon. James Bowdoin,
John Hancock, Esq.,
Joseph Green, Esq.,
Richard Carey, Esq.,
Mr. John Wheatley, her master,
The Rev. Charles Chauncy, D.D.,
The Rev. Mather Byles, D.D.,
The Rev. Ed. Pemberton, D.D.,
The Rev. Andrew Elliot, D.D.,
The Rev. Samuel Cooper, D.D.,
The Rev. Mr. Samuel Mather,
The Rev. Mr. John Morehead.

I

THE FIRST STANZA

But here I sit, and mourn a grov'ling mind
That fain would mount, and ride upon the wind.
To Maecenas

CHAPTER ONE

A Small Bit of Black Ivory

Boston awoke as usual that morning—to the ringing of bells. Hardly had the stars faded when cowbells began to sound as those faithful ones, having contributed warm, foamy milk for the breakfast table, made off for the crisp, fresh grass and blueberry bushes on the Commons. It was Market Day and at six o'clock the great bell in Dock Square announced its opening and the tinkle, tinkle of doorbells on all sides bore witness to thrifty wives and maidens setting forth for first choice of merchandise. Vendors were ringing hand bells in the street, advertising wonders and sales, and then schoolmasters filled the air with the clanging of their bells, hastening laggers on their way to school. Indeed, Boston offered little quiet for sleepyheads on that June morning in 1761.

Harbor bells were still muted in the early morning mist when a big gray ship nosed its way cautiously among the islands. It came silent as a ghost ship out of the night and was a battered, unwashed thing from which respectable whalers, sloops and schooners shied away. As it slipped through the narrow channel between Castle and Governor's islands, the English flag floating above the fort, drooped for a moment and the laughter of the sea gulls took on a ferocious eagerness. The sailor piloting the ship gazed unblinkingly ahead, but he wanted to shout for joy, for at last he was back home. Soon he would leave this cursed ship forever!

Boston, most prosperous town in the New World, reached like a finger far out into the water. The three big hills rose like fortress towers and the valleys were covered with chimneys from which fluttered tatters of smoke like flags of welcome. But to the pilot the church steeples pointed accusing fingers to the sky and the mass of piers, shipyards, distilleries and wharves ranged the town like soldiers on guard.

He brought the ship in without mishap, docking so close to the Old Feather store that the prow almost touched its side; then without a backward glance he slowly made his way to the rail and, climbing overboard, dropped on to the almost deserted wharf. For this sailor was a Boston man;

4

he wanted to get off the ship and away so that no one would know he had shipped on a slaver. He fled from his disgrace but he could not escape the knowledge of what was going on behind him.

They were prying open the hatches, loosing such sights and sounds and smells as would stagger hardier souls than the young pilot. Human beings had been packed and chained and fastened in that hole for three long months. Water had been passed down and food tossed into the hole but no one on the ship had dared go down. At first the screaming and shouting and wailing had gone on day and night. After a time the awful silence was even more horrible. Of course on every trip much of the cargo "spoiled" but what was left brought a good price. For slavers were men who kidnaped black people in Africa and brought them all the way across the seas to be sold as slaves in America. They referred to themselves as traders in "black ivory." So many of the Africans died on the way that losses were heavy. It was a nasty business, avoided by decent seamen. So before the people of the town were astir the young sailor had lost himself in the jumble of warehouses and dram-shops surrounding the piers. He resolved to choose his next ship more carefully.

It was one of those first June mornings, when after several days of brisk showers everything is clean and sweet. Mrs. Susannah Wheatley viewed the world through her crisp, white curtains and decided to accompany her husband into "the city"

5

to do some marketing. So instead of Mr. Wheatley setting off right after breakfast for a brisk walk down King Street to Queen and along Pudding-lane to the Mall he had Black Prince bring around the chaise and they drove off in style. John Wheatley was a prosperous tailor-merchant. His two bright young apprentices would take down the shutters and open the shop. He could afford to indulge his worthy wife while she went about her errands.

Marketing combined business with pleasure for Mrs. Wheatley. The stalls at the lower end of Charles Street, piled high with vegetables, fruit, fish and flowers, delighted her eyes. Everybody went to market at one time or another so there was always the chance of meeting a friend and there were always bargains; chickens squawked, ducks quacked and squealing little pigs darted about. On market days merchants all along the way lined the sidewalks with tables displaying their wares. It was necessary to leave the chaise and wander up and down between stalls and voluble hucksters, buying something here and something there—trying not to miss anything. After two hours of such dalliance poor Mr. Wheatley was thoroughly exhausted.

"My dear," Mr. Wheatley spoke firmly, "I'm sure Prince has collected your bundles and is waiting to drive you home. I must be getting to the store."

"One moment, John." Mrs. Wheatley was fingering a lustrous piece of brocade heaped in a tempting pile on a table. The merchant seeing her pause in front of his door hurried out.

"A bargain, ma'am!" he beamed upon them. "Only five shillings for the length!"

Some attraction at the end of the street was crowding the sidewalk. A boy carrying a huge basket bumped against Mrs. Wheatley as she hesitated.

"Take care there, fellow!" Mr. Wheatley waved his cane threateningly. "Can't you see the lady?" The culprit ducked out of the way but the pressure of the crowd increased. Mr. Wheatley turned to his wife.

"Come! I'll take you to the chaise. Let's get out of this."

Mrs. Wheatley relinquished the brocade with a little sigh. She was a dutiful wife and John a good husband. He was not, however, given to extravagances and she didn't really need the dress length. Her hand in his arm they began making their way as rapidly as the crowd would permit. Ahead someone was shouting in a loud, raucous voice.

"What is it? What's that man saying?" Mrs. Wheatley was straining her neck trying to see.

"Come this way!" her husband admonished. "It's a slave auction. Don't go that way!"

"But Prince is on that corner," Mrs. Wheatley protested. "That's where I told him to wait." Mrs. Wheatley was pushing her way in the direction of the open square. All around she heard comments.

"A blight on slavers!" A carpenter with his tools glared around him.

"Mamma, I wanna see!" A little boy pulled at his mother's skirts, but she jerked him to one side with "Hush, Tommy, 'tis wicked. Come along!"

Now they could see the auction block in the middle of the square. The auctioneer urged the hesitating passers-by to come forward.

"Here! Here! Here! Best imported black ivory. Fresh load. Straight off the boat!"

"I don't see Prince." Mr. Wheatley's eyes were searching the square but no waiting chaise was in sight. "Now where could that fellow have gone?"

But Mrs. Wheatley was staring in horror at the group of slaves huddled behind the block. Near by stood huge, scowling keepers with long, black whips in their hands. John Wheatley felt his wife clutching his arm.

"Here, my dear, never mind Prince. Don't look at them. We'll go this way!" He was endeavoring to lead her away. But Mrs. Wheatley held back.

"No, no, John! Let's not run away. They're human beings."

"Blimy! What a filthy lot!" A prospective buyer studied the lot. "I'll wager they've got the fever!"

"Nonsense, sir." The auctioneer spoke briskly. "They still rollin' with the ship. Be perk as colts in a couple of days." One of the slaves made a move and his chains rattled. "Here you, there, look sharp!" The auctioneer called quickly to a keeper.

8

The long whip curled out and fell on the naked shoulders. The black man leaped and snarled like a trapped animal. The auctioneer spoke proudly. "See! Plenty of spirit in that young buck!"

"John, it's horrible!"

"Come away, my dear." Mr. Wheatley was overcome with helplessness. He saw that his wife was about to faint but still she clung stubbornly to his arm, refusing to budge. At that moment the auctioneer had reached behind him and, picking up a small object, stood it on the block. At the sight a boy on the square gave a shout of laughter.

"Look at that," he pointed, "a little naked savage!"

The auctioneer grinned. "Right you are. Fine as a suckling pig!"

"John! It's a little girl!"

This was the auctioneer's joke. Business was not going too well so he injected this "toy" into the proceedings.

"Here's a cute gift for your lady, sirs! Sound as a fiddle! Look at this smooth skin. Not more than five or six. At this age they're bright as monkeys and can be trained for anything!"

Her eyes were squeezed tight and she shivered in the morning sunshine. Her feet, cut by the cobble stones, curled inward, her hands groped for some familiar softness, while her whimpering was that of a terrified, young animal.

"It's senseless to bring them that young," Mr. Wheatley grumbled, trying to fill the starkness of

Susannah Wheatley's stillness. He could feel her tremble as she stood there staring.

"Is it dumb?" A rakish young fop eyed the small piece with a speculative eye.

"Aha! Want to hear the monkey squeal?" asked the auctioneer. He brought his hand down with a resounding smack on the little girl's bottom. She cried out in pain.

"Oh, John!" Mrs. Wheatley's voice expressed her own anguish.

"Why don't you come away?" Mr. Wheatley looked in every direction. If only he could spy Prince or the chaise!

Now they heard a man's voice bidding: "I'll give ten shillings for it."

"Come now, sir!" The auctioneer was being very persuasive.

"John! John, I want to buy her!"

Mr. Wheatley stared at his wife in amazement. "You! You would buy a slave on auction. The idea!"

"But John, somebody's going to buy her. Look there at that awful woman."

A coarse-faced, frowzy woman had approached the block and was turning the child around and examining her.

"You'll find plenty of work in her, madam," encouraged the auctioneer. "Buy cheap now and train her yourself."

"One pound!" bid the woman in a hoarse voice.

"No! No!" Mrs. Wheatley protested and then called in a firm voice, "One pound, half!"

"Stop this nonsense!" Mr. Wheatley was rapidly losing patience. "She's wild! What can you do with her?"

"Two pounds!" called out the other woman.

"Gentlemen!" Now the auctioneer was beaming. "Are you going to let these ladies pick up this trick for a mere song?"

"I'll give two pounds, half!" called one of the men who had just come up. He turned to a friend accompanying him. "You know, it's all the rage in London to dress them up and sit them on the box when driving out. It's quite an idea!"

Mrs. Wheatley was twisting her hands. She didn't want to anger her husband but the words were forced from her.

"Three pounds!" she shouted.

There was a moment of silence. People were staring at her now and there was some laughter. The auctioneer eyed the crowd. He had to get on with the business at hand.

"Do I hear another bid? No? Well—going—going—*gone* to the lady with the rose ruffles!"

Mrs. Wheatley did not dare look up. What to do now? Of course she didn't have three pounds in her purse. A movement in the crowd carried them along with the others. John Wheatley had said nothing, but she was gratefully conscious that her arm was still in his. Perhaps he was not too angry! She raised her eyes to the block. The child had disappeared. A black man in chains was being dragged forward and the auctioneer was again shouting, "Step this way, gentlemen! Here we have a good, strong buck. . . ."

She saw the fellow bringing her the child and could only stare.

"You the lady bought it, ma'am?"

Waves of gratitude swept over her when Mr. Wheatley spoke.

"Yes!" He was fumbling in his wallet. "Here you are, three pounds."

"Thankee, sir!" said the man. Then turning to Mrs. Wheatley: "Here 'tis! Lay hold to this string. I tied it round her middle. Hold fast!"

The small, black creature's eyes were still squeezed tight. Curious folks had formed a circle around them. Mrs. Wheatley swallowed with embarrassment.

"Can—can she talk?" She asked the question as she tried desperately to cope with the situation.

The clerk snorted. "Talk! Lady, she just been picked off a tree! She don't know *nothing!*" Several people laughed and the fellow bounced off well pleased with himself.

Then at last Mr. Wheatley addressed himself to his lady. His voice was cool.

"Well, Mrs. Wheatley, now that you've finished your marketing it appears I'll have to see you home. We certainly can't stand all morning in this square."

For the first time Mrs. Wheatley remembered

12

that they had come here expecting to find Prince with the chaise. But all she could see in the square were people milling around the slave block. And here she stood clutching a piece of cord to which was attached a tiny human being shrunk into itself, with bent head and arms wrapped around trembling body so that she could hardly see what it looked like. Caught in her own dilemma the good lady lifted her eyes to her husband and spoke meekly.

"Yes, dear."

He turned and started back toward the street, not waiting to hear Mrs. Wheatley's hesitant question, "How can I—?" and then panic making her speak sharply, "Come along, girl."

"You gotta jerk the string!" an onlooker informed her. He stepped forward. "Here, I'll show you." Seizing the cord in his own hand he gave it a sudden, quick pull.

"Oh, no!" The cry was wrung from Mrs. Wheatley as the child almost fell to the ground.

"See, that does it," the man handed her the cord. "Now, she's moving."

Mrs. Wheatley's distress was such that she did not thank him. Instead, with a quick movement she stripped the kerchief from about her neck and, bending, wrapped it around the trembling body. Then pulling gently at the string she moved toward her husband. He was waiting for her on the corner. He wanted to laugh at his wife's flushed face and the picture she made leading her purchase. He

13

turned away for one last, searching glance up and down the street.

"Drat that Prince," Mr. Wheatley's irritation was evident. "This is a fine time for him to disappear!" His wife's contrite face was too much for him. Once more he tucked her hand inside his arm and said, "Well, come along, my dear." Then he smiled. "The townspeople will gossip this morning. Mistress Wheatley leading a slave through the streets!"

"Oh, John!" was all the good lady could say.

CHAPTER TWO

"Your Name is Phillis"

The jerk on the tight cord had hurt, but then came the warm touch of human hands and blood began trickling into cold, rigid limbs. With the passing of the hands there remained a sweet softness all about her body. The child allowed the breath she had been holding in cramped lungs to escape, her tiny hand moved furtively until the fingers could curl about the softness. Then she dared to open her eyes a little. They were leading her away. This much was clear. What would happen now? As the horrible noises were left behind she cautiously peered about. Ugliness! Ugliness all around—like a ravaged valley after a storm—hard, queer ugliness everywhere. She closed her

15

eyes and stumbled along. The hardness hurt her feet, but she was glad they were leading her away from the black hole.

They were discussing the disappearance of Prince and the chaise.

"You don't suppose he's being held some-where?" Mrs. Wheatley's voice expressed anxiety. This was not like Prince and she knew that slaves were frequently picked up for real or fancied mis-demeanors, to the great embarrassment and incon-venience of their masters. Any accusation against the slave was accepted. Mrs. Wheatley knew that Prince was not as docile as he might be. His "talking back" could easily get him into trouble.

"I suppose he was ordered away from the square because of the slave auction." This had just oc-curred to Mr. Wheatley.

"Why, of course," Mrs. Wheatley took up this explanation. "And you can't blame him for hurry-ing away, now can you, John?"

But Mr. Wheatley refused to commit himself on that point. He had lost the full morning as well as thrown away three pounds. He looked back at their small purchase. Three pounds!

"If we can only slip into the house without being seen," Mrs. Wheatley sighed softly. "Oh, dear, there's Mrs. Pembrock!" The lady had looked up from trimming her roses and was staring in their direction. Mrs. Wheatley called out brightly, "Good morning, Mrs. Pembrock!"

At the sound of the cheery call the child opened

her eyes once more. They had just turned the corner into King Street with its avenue of spreading chestnut trees, green yards and comfortable, sprawling houses sitting behind clipped hedges and flower gardens. The child stood transfixed while joy poured over her in a stream, for here at last she saw familiar beauty. Trees! Green earth! She sniffed the fragrance of the roses.

"Ah—e—e!" They did not hear the little murmur of gladness. And to the child's amazement, they continued to walk on the rough hardness when all around lay patches of beautiful green! The gentle tugging on the rope held her in place. But now her eyes were opened wide and when they turned in and she spied the loveliness of climbing red roses she broke away.

"John!" Mrs. Wheatley cried out in alarm.

The rope trailing behind her, the little figure sped across the lawn toward the rose trellis and disappeared inside the mass of green.

"Why didn't you hold on?" Mr. Wheatley demanded as they hurried after her. The leaves quivered as they approached and black eyes stared up at them.

"She's hugging the stems and they'll cut her. But look at her face. She's happy and I do believe she's trying to sing!"

It was true. A crooning sound came from the half-parted lips. The child buried her face in the flowers. She felt the prick of the thorns but it was good—good. Her flesh pressed against the good,

17

soft earth and all the horror was gone. For she was back home again. She had found her way.

> Burrow deep into the earth
> And soon ma-ma will come again
> Lay the ear close down and listen
> Listen for the beating of the drums
> Make a song of gladness to the earth
> Like a drum.

It was her song and she made it out of thanksgiving for deliverance from the black hole. But the strange grownups bending over her did not understand.

From inside the house came a girl's voice: "Is that you, Mother?"

Fifteen-year-old Mary Wheatley appeared on the porch and regarded her parents with some surprise.

"Father, dear! I should not expect to see you home at this hour? May I ask what you are doing?"

"Come, Mary, and help your mother." Mary heard the annoyance in her father's voice. "She's bought a slave at a street auction and now let it get away!"

"Mother!" Mary could not believe her ears. She ran down the steps.

"There—there she is." Mrs. Wheatley pointed to the quivering leaves.

"Well, my dear," Mr. Wheatley spoke briskly to

his wife, "I've accompanied you home. I must get to the shop. Call Sukey!" he admonished. "She'll know what to do." And he was off down the gravel path and out the white picket gate.

As he turned the corner he met Black Prince!

"A fine time for you to be showing yourself!" Mr. Wheatley struck the walk with his cane and glared.

Prince halted the horse and sat with the reins slack, his head hanging down.

"Massa—" he began and stopped.

"Well, well, speak up!" Mr. Wheatley commanded.

Prince's explanation was involved. He said that when he heard a slave ship had come in that morning he decided to slip down to the docks while Mrs. Wheatley was doing her marketing.

"Might be somebody I knowed," he explained, looking off into the distance.

It was the old story. Slaves who themselves had been captured and brought from far across the seas looking—vainly, fearfully hoping—for one familiar face among other groups of slaves.

For a moment Mr. Wheatley said nothing. Then he cleared his throat and blurted out, "Well, be off with you!" He hurried on to his shop.

From a distance young Nathaniel Wheatley, returning from Latin School, saw his father wave the chaise homeward and go off on foot. He thought Mr. Wheatley was dismissing Black Prince because he preferred to walk.

19

"Ahoy, Prince!" called Nat, running forward. "Ah," he said, "I'll ride home today."

Black Prince grinned and waited until the young man had clambered up on the high seat beside him.

Nathaniel and Mary were twins though they resembled each other very little. The boy was stocky and dark while Mary was slender and very blond but the close tie between them was always apparent. They were a perfect team, each complimenting the other.

Mrs. Wheatley would have stared had she seen her son arriving in the chaise for which she had vainly searched, but she and Mary were so intent upon trying to devise some method of getting the little black girl out of the bushes that she was only aware of his presence when he called, "Pray, what are you two doing?"

"Look!" Mary parted the leaves so that her brother could see the crouching child. "Mother bought her!" Nat stared in astonishment.

"Children, there was no other way." Mrs. Wheatley had recovered the rope and now tugged at it, but the child only wrapped her arms around the roots of the vine and could not be budged. Her head was pressed hard against the earth so that her face was hidden.

"They were auctioning her off on the block," Mrs. Wheatley continued. "She was so tiny and helpless."

20

"Of course, Mother, we understand." Mary spoke soothingly.

"Jupiter!" The boy was exclaiming. "A real African!"

"She's frightened to death. Here, Nat, break off a spray and offer it to her. Maybe she'll understand we don't want to hurt her."

The child felt the leaves with their fragrant buds against her cheek. She turned her head and saw the hand extending the branch. The hand was strange but a green branch extended this way meant friendship. This she knew well. So she stretched out her hand and took the twig.

"Look, Nat!" Mary's voice sang. "She's smiling!"

The twig was sweet. The child shifted her position so that she could hold it up to the sun. This, too, was proper when friends met.

"As if it's some sort of ceremony," Nat was observing the gesture. "That spray means something special to her."

"I'm sure she'll come out now, Mother," Mary knelt on the ground and parted the vines.

The child looked up into a face that was strangely beautiful. It was like the flowers that grow in the deep grass—pale and gold—with bits of blue brightness like pieces of the sky. Shyly the dark little hand extended the twig toward the lovely face.

"There's a Greek name for 'green bough.' Phillis

comes from the word. Maybe we'll have to clothe her in green boughs. She certainly likes them."

"Phillis!" Mary spoke softly, smiling at the child. "We'll call you Phillis! See, the spray is yours. You can keep it. Put your hand in mine. Come, Phillis!"

The child understood the singing sweetness in the voice. Gratefully she curled her fingers about the soft, white hand which tugged gently until she stood upright on the grass. Mrs. Wheatley's broad kerchief lay caught in the bushes.

"Quick, now. Take her around to Aunt Sukey and tell her to give her a good tubbing. I'll find some clothes."

The Wheatleys had three slaves, though they would have indignantly repudiated the system. Aunt Sukey had been with Susannah Wheatley's family since Mrs. Wheatley was a girl and had gone with her young mistress to her new home on King Street. There she had organized the house and nursed the twins through many ailments. Now she was old and did little work, though she continued to keep a sharp eye on everything and would countenance no "sass" from the children. Lima was a very black Portuguese woman. Mr. Wheatley had come across her one evening down on the wharves where she was begging for work, declaring that she was "va' strong" and "good cook." It was evident that she had escaped from one of the ships, but as she showed signs of horrible abuse, he gave her shelter in the shop and later took her

22

home where she proved to be even better than her word. "Board and keep" was all she asked for long and faithful work and she soon slipped into a permanent place in the kitchen. Black Prince, the third slave, was a different matter. Mr. Wheatley had obtained him through a business transaction which he always suspected as being shady. Prince was a well-proportioned, intelligent young fellow. After a time master and slave entered into a bargain whereby the slave would buy his own freedom. Prince did all sorts of odd jobs during his spare time. In rush seasons he worked in the tailor shop and Mr. Wheatley paid him a small wage. But time was passing and the slave had not been able to "put by" enough to pay the price. Meanwhile, except for occasional sullen fits and some "impudence," Black Prince worked well, though his heart was not in it.

"He all et up fur da freedom!" Aunt Sukey, watching him, made the comment. Big Lima only shook her head. After the passing of the years the two old women knew that freedom was not for them. But they did not believe Black Prince would die a slave.

This June day Sukey was sunning herself under the grape arbor, placidly smoking her pipe. It fell from between her gums when Mary rounded the house, leading her small charge.

"Blessed Jesus!" the old lady exclaimed. "What's dat?"

"Isn't she nice? Look at her, Aunt Sukey. She's

23

not afraid, she's holding tight to my hand!" Mary was delighted with her success.

"Where yo git dat naked child, honey? Fo' Gawd, she look like a wild savage!"

"Mother bought her—on the street. Think of it, Aunt Sukey, they were selling this poor little thing— all by herself."

"Ain't she got no mammy?" Aunt Sukey had hobbled forward and was untying the cord. As a rule young children were sold only with their mothers, but as Sukey well knew, there were many exceptions.

The child sniffed the old one. True, she had the face of people but the smell was quite different. She was most certainly of a distant tribe, for the tongue was strange. Things began to dance queerly and a great heaviness seemed to fall on her. Aunt Sukey reached out and caught the child as she swayed.

They forced a drop of brandy between the clenched teeth, then warm water and a little food. The child was famished, of course, but care had to be taken in this. She thought the end had come when they brought the steaming, wooden tub and cried pitifully. But Aunt Sukey was well versed in such matters. Her hands were gentle though firm and after a time the little body relaxed in the cleansing suds. Then they wrapped her up in something warm. Aunt Sukey sent Mary to the well for the hollowed gourd hanging there. Instead of pouring the broth into a bowl she poured it into the

24

gourd, handing it to the child when it had cooled a little. The little black face lighted up.

"See!" Aunt Sukey nodded her head. "Dis she know. Her mammy use gourd for feedin'."

The child gulped down the liquid and smacked her lips. Ah! It was good.

"She shall sleep in my room, Mother," Mary was saying. "Give her to me for my very own. Please, Mother!"

"I'm not sure your father would—" began Mrs. Wheatley.

"Ah, Mother, we can train her!" Nat always joined with Mary in any undertaking. "She has to learn to talk and everything. We'll teach her."

For want of a better solution, so it was decided. Nat brought a box in from the barn and lined it with fresh hay. They made up a little bed in one corner of Mary's room.

"Do you think she'll try to run away?" Mary asked her brother anxiously.

"Anybody can see she likes you already!" Brother Nat assured. "We'll keep giving her flowers and greens. That's going to be her talisman, remember."

"Oh, you and your Greek stories," teased the sister.

But the memory etched indelibly on the child's mind of these days was the lovely pale face all framed with gold bending over her and the soft, sweet voice saying, "Phillis! Your name is Phillis."

Reading, Writing and 'Rithmetic

CHAPTER THREE

Reading, Writing and 'Rithmetic

So Mary Wheatley
stretched out her hand and picked a human bud
that had been tossed among the rocks of New
England. She transplanted it into her home and
heart and tended it carefully.

Mary had soon tired of dolls. She preferred her
brother's games. Then as books became important
to Nat he shared them with his twin sister. So it
happened that Mary Wheatley had more education
than most fifteen-year-old girls in Boston at a time
when it was not uncommon for a girl even in one
of the better families to be unable to write. Girls
who did not have to work stayed at home and
learned cooking, housekeeping and needlework

26

from their mothers. The more fortunate were given a year or two of "finishing" in the Young Ladies Seminary. But boys were either apprenticed to a craftsman from whom they learned a trade, or were sent to school.

Sons of artisans and shopkeepers usually went to writing schools where they also learned arithmetic and enough about geography to trace a ship's course. But John Wheatley had decided to make a clergyman of his son. Nat was therefore sent to a Latin school which would prepare him for Harvard College. These Latin schools introduced young gentlemen to the classics, grounded them in Latin and Greek, the principles of Euclid and the discourses of Thomas Aquinas. Nat unburdened himself to the always-sympathetic Mary. If she failed to grasp all that he endeavored to impart she nevertheless was far more interested in books than she was in crocheting or candlemaking. Her mother had been growing a little anxious.

"It's not *ladylike*," Mrs. Wheatley sighed, envisioning a "bookish" Mary neglected and unwed.

Now to her mother's delight all this was changed. Mary's devotion to the black child was complete.

"She's simply wonderful with the little thing!" Mrs. Wheatley reported to her husband.

"That's fine! That's fine, my dear!" Mr. Wheatley's thoughts were down on the wharves. All Boston merchants were worried these days. After a period of prosperity produced by supplying materials and ships and men for England to drive the French out of America, the mother country was now bankrupting New England by enforcing certain of the Navigation Acts. Mr. Wheatley had little time for attention to the petty vanities of the females in his household.

Aunt Sukey was not given to flattery, but even she had to acknowledge that the African child was bright. Black Prince was more emphatic.

"Dat chile's got *sense!*" Prince spoke proudly. "An' Miss Mary givin' huh *white* folk's teachin'."

"Hush you' mouf!" cautioned Big Lima.

The three slaves peered through the kitchen door out into the garden where they could see Mary and the child. Prince had brought down from the attic Mary's own little rocking chair and put it under the big elm tree. In it the child was now rocking blissfully as she had seen Mrs. Wheatley and Aunt Sukey do. Mary's laughter sounded with a silver tinkle.

"All right, Phillis—enough of rocking." Mary sat on a stone bench, a table strewn with papers and books in front of her. Now she placed her finger on the table, fixed her eyes sternly on the child and asked, "What am I touching?"

"Rocky! Rocky! Rocky!" The small one made a song, rocking in rhythm to her words.

"No, Phillis!" At the sharp command the child stopped and her eyes grew large.

"Hear me, now!" Once more Mary made a large gesture of pressing her finger against the table. "Tell me. What do I touch?"

The child's attention was focused. For a moment she was very still, her eyes wrinkled. Then her lips formed a syllable.

"Wa—" she stopped, watching Mary's face. And Mary shook her head.

"What is this, Phillis?" Mary asked again, unhurried, patient. "Remember, I told you yesterday. Ta—" she started the word and stopped.

At this a broad smile spread over the little dark face.

"Tay—bah!" she shouted the word triumphantly.

"Table! That's it, Phillis, that's it!"

In the kitchen the three slaves also exhaled with relief and went about their work. Black Prince whistled as he walked toward the stable.

There was the first time the large gray cat from next door appeared in the garden and the child cried out in alarm.

"Afraid, Phillis? Afraid of the nice pussycat?" Phillis was trembling. Some memory of other cats stirred in her mind. Mary's voice reassured—she did not run but her eyes were watchful. Then Mary leaned over and stroked the cat gently, saying, "Nice kitty! See, Phillis, she won't hurt you!"

And the memory of the jungle cat faded. Phillis smiled. She came closer. Finally the child entended her hand and said, "Kitty?"

"Yes, kitty. Here—stroke her!" Mary guided the little hand with her own. "Isn't she soft and nice?"

And the child agreed, "Nice!" After a time she likewise lost her fear of the dark.

There was another memory which remained with Phillis all her life.

Mary did not know what woke her that morning, for she was not conscious of hearing anything. But her eyes opened and she lay there a moment realizing it was the gray of early dawn showing through her window. The night had been oppressively hot; the curtains hung limp and the twittering of the birds outside was subdued. Mary turned and looked over toward the child's box. It was empty!

In a moment Mary was out of bed. She threw a robe over her thin nightdress and was out in the hall. She could hear nothing but the ticking of the big clock in the shadows below. Mary hesitated a moment. Should she wake Nat? Surely the child was in the house. There was nothing to be alarmed about—yet.

Downstairs was hot and close but the door leading to the back of the house was open, which seemed to suggest that someone might have passed that way. Kitchen doors were seldom locked and when Mary saw this door standing ajar she was certain Phillis had gone through into the garden. She stepped out into the paved kitchen yard. Then she heard someone at the well. She heard the bucket knocking against the stones and the splash of water.

The well, really a spring caught in a rock basin, was beyond the garden. As soon as she rounded the stable she saw Phillis. The child's long, white cotton nightdress was now soiled and wet from her struggle with the big bucket. But she had managed to draw up some water and was now emptying it into one of Big Lima's earthen kitchen bowls. Mary checked the call which rose to her lips and stopped. There was a queer intentness about the child's movements. Surely she was not going to all this trouble to get a drink of water. A pail of water with a handy dipper always stood on the kitchen table. And why had she taken the bowl? Mary stood behind the hedge—waiting.

It was as if the whole dew-drenched garden was holding its breath. Everything was heavy with dew and for the moment the twittering of the birds had ceased. Then Mary saw the child walk slowly up the little knoll at the edge of the lot. She walked holding the bowl of water extended in her hands. When she came to the fence she raised the bowl above her head, and she, too, seemed to be waiting. It was only for a moment. Suddenly Mary realized what was happening—the sun was rising! All the birds and the flowers in the garden knew it, too. The small black girl was facing the sun and as the first bright streak shot across the sky she tipped her bowl and let the water pour to the ground in an even stream. Then while Mary continued to gaze in astonishment the child began to move forward, backward in a pattern of steps which finally encircled the spot. And as she moved she sang so softly that the sound reached Mary only as part of the chorus in the waking garden.

It was over in a few moments. The child seemed to incline her head and backed away through the garden toward the hedge where Mary was standing. When she was close by, Mary spoke softly so as not to startle her.

"Phillis!"

Mary saw the radiance in the little black face when it turned to her. Then it drained away and before Mary could put out her hand the earthen bowl slipped and crashed on the stone walk. The child stared at it in horror, burst into tears and ran through the kitchen door into the house.

Mary was bewildered. She felt guilty, as if she had done something frightfully wrong. She stooped and picked up the broken pieces of the bowl while she tried to adjust her thoughts. *Phillis had never run away from her before!* What did this mean? She was certain now that there was some meaning. A feeling of anxiety swept over her regarding this child—this dark stranger in their midst. She hurried into the house and up to her room. Would the child be there?

She had slipped out of the soggy, wet gown and sat huddled in the corner, her arms wrapped about her naked body. Mary did not see her on the slave auction block but Mrs. Wheatley would have recognized the same body position, the same shrinking away into herself. Only the black eyes moved, watching Mary but revealing nothing. Mary decided on a course of action. She kicked off her soft slippers and took off her robe.

"I'm sleepy, Phillis. Go back to bed!" Then, as if it were an afterthought, she pointed to the box where they kept Phillis' few clothes, and said, "Put on a clean gown."

Mary lay down on her bed and turned her back on the child. For a while there was no movement. Mary pretended to be asleep. When she heard the crackle of paper she knew the child was obeying and that a crisis had passed.

Nat was able to give some explanation.

"I tell you the child was carrying on some African ceremony that had to do with the rising of the sun. This is common among primitive peoples. Maybe her folks were sun worshipers."

"But why was she afraid of *me?*" Mary's tone expressed her own hurt.

"She was confused. You see, she's all right now!"

Not until Phillis was able to express herself clearly in English did Mary completely understand. But it was as Nat had said. The one clear memory which no amount of terror or darkness eliminated from the little African's mind was that of her mother going out early in the morning to "pour water" to the sun.

As time passed, the compulsion of this memory

ceased. And when she began to put words together young Nat himself took a hand. On a day when it was too cool to sit in the garden Nat was saying:

"Now say after me, Phillis—I see a chair."

"I—see—a chair." Phillis looked rather unhappily toward Mary who nodded encouragement.

"I see a man." Nat spoke faster, more briskly than Mary had been doing.

Phillis imitated her new teacher and spoke quickly, "I see man."

"I see an apple."

Instead of responding, Phillis looked hard at the table and then asked, "Where apple?"

Mary gave a peal of laughter. "You see, Nat, *I* don't use regular copybook methods. If I say, I see an apple, I really mean it."

"Well," Nat defended his method, "she might as well learn what a sentence is. After all, we're not really talking about apples."

"Oh, but we *are*. Anyhow, Phillis, here's an apple on the sideboard. Now say it."

Phillis had been following the verbal exchange with her bright eyes. She was beginning to understand much of what she heard. Now she smiled and said, "I see apple."

"Do you see a book?" asked Nat.

Phillis nodded her head vigorously, "Yes, yes . . . sir, I see a book."

"Now, Phillis, what do you want? Say, I want—"

Phillis interrupted with, "I want apple."

Nat burst out laughing this time. "Good for

you, Phillis," he said. Then to Mary, "Already she asks for apples. Well, give it to her! She earned it."

Mary's tone expressed her disappointment. "I was hoping she would ask for a book."

"You forget, my dear sister," Nat spoke like a young man of the world, "the primitive puts first things first."

CHAPTER FOUR

This Child Has a Mind

The year 1765 began unhappily. Early in January whispers started that dreaded smallpox was in the town. When the *News-Letter* reported two deaths from this disease, notices were posted announcing that the selectmen would permit inoculation by "gentlemen physicians" and that "Small Pox Gratis will be given to poor inhabitants." People remembering the scourge of 1721, when thousands in the colony died, knew the authorities were desperate. Vaccination, which finally defeated this ancient terror of mankind, had not been discovered. The inoculation was dangerous both to the patient and to the community, for the "light case" it was supposed to produce often proved fatal and it was at all times contagious.

As the word spread, everybody who could fled to the country. Day and night carts rumbled over the cobbles as townspeople abandoned their houses and trades to get out of the infested seaport.

"You must take Mary and go!" Mr. Wheatley urged his wife. "Nat is quite safe at Cambridge."

But the usually gentle Mrs. Wheatley shook her head. "We will not go away and leave you, John."

Phillis heard about it first from Black Prince. As was her habit, she appeared in the kitchen early one morning to obtain a pitcher of warm water for her mistress. Prince had just brought in an armful of wood for the stove on which Big Lima was preparing the first meal of the day. The kitchen was warm and odorous and bright with colored pottery. Phillis lingered over her errand.

"Is it cold today, Prince?" She pressed her face against the windowpane, looking out at the frozen whiteness. "I hope the sun shines a little, just a little today." She spoke anxiously.

"Why? Why yo' hope dat?" Prince regarded her steadily.

"Cause Miss Mary say—if it's nice day—we're going into town." She beamed. "I love to go in town with Miss Mary!"

Prince frowned. "No! yo'all dassent set foot outside dis house! I tell Miss Mary."

37

"Prince!" Phillis regarded the dark giant with amazement.

Aunt Sukey, comfortably enthroned in her rocking chair behind the stove, looked up from the tray of apples she was peeling:

"Min' yo' bisness, mahn!"

Black Prince turned on the old lady. "Yo' dar, croaking by da fire! What yo' know? Wan' see dis chile come down wid da pox? Wan' see all Miss Mary's pretty face scarred?"

While the two women and Phillis listened with growing horror, Black Prince told them of "da pox." He had seen the disease fastening itself upon the poor of Boston and he left out none of the gruesome details.

"Dat's why I gonna tell Miss Mary," he concluded.

"No! No, Prince!" It was Phillis now, clinging to his arm, pleading. "Don't tell her. I won't let her go out! I'll look out for her!"

Prince regarded the child fondly. It was nearly four years now since they had brought her home. He was proud of her growth, of her good manners and "white folks learnin'."

"How yo' stop Miss Mary?" he asked.

"I don't know. I can't say this minute. But I will. I'll think *hard* and find a way."

Prince shook himself free. "Aw right," he said sternly, "think!" He went out and chuckled to himself as he made his way across the icy yard.

Phillis' arms trembled as she bore the filled

pitcher to the second floor. She could hear the master's voice behind the closed door of his bedroom. She filled the bowls in the dressing room hurriedly, grateful for the fact that he had not come out. Then she made her way down the hall to Mary's room. Mary was up and standing beside the blazing fire. The years had brought the too-thin, rather tomboyish girl to lovely womanhood. And it was in this gracious image that her adoring little acolyte sought to shape herself.

"Good morning, Phillis. Look! The sun is shining! How could you be late on such a beautiful morning?"

"Good morning, Miss Mary!" Phillis poured the water and arranged the towels with careful attention to each detail. If only a storm were raging! Instead, now bright sunshine was transforming all the outside world into glistening beauty.

"We'll take lessons right after breakfast," Mary continued gaily. "If you are *very* good perhaps we'll have time to. . . ." She broke off to regard Phillis with alarm. The little girl was bent over in a paroxysm of coughing. "Why, Phillis, I didn't know you had a cold!"

"Yes . . . ma'am . . . last night . . . I. . . ." Phillis seemed to struggle for breath.

Mary knew the difficulties they had encountered in trying to adjust this child from a warmer climate to the rigors of New England weather. The first two winters had been very hazardous, during the third things had gone easier, while so far this fourth winter Phillis had seemed quite able to cope with the weather. How on earth could she have caught such a bad cold overnight? Mary sighed and then spoke very gently:

"That will do, Phillis. Perhaps you'd better go lie down. I think I'll send Prince for the doctor."

"Oh, no, Miss Mary!" Phillis' alarm was not feigned. "I'll—I'll be all right. It was just my throat."

"Stick out your tongue, Phillis!" Mary studied the small, red protrusion. "Um—um," she said. "Maybe a good dose of bitters will straighten you out." Phillis shivered with apprehension but she dared not protest. "Go down to the kitchen and keep warm. I'll be down in a few minutes and have Aunt Sukey mix you a dose."

So they did not go downtown that day nor that week. And Phillis took her bitters like a little Spartan and remembered to cough at intervals. Black Prince regarded her with pride. Once he managed to slip her a sweet.

But in spite of Phillis' efforts the smallpox came to the Wheatley household. No one ever knew how. On a gray February evening when Mr. Wheatley returned from his shop he was met by a guard stationed in front of his house. When he saw the flag hanging above the door his face blanched.

"God have mercy!" The stricken man gasped a fervent prayer and the guard took his arm.

"Bear up, man!" he said. "'Tis one of the servants. But we had to quarantine them all. Here is a letter from your wife."

It was too dark to read the letter on the street. For a moment John Wheatley just stood there, staring about rather wildly. Then he sighted the apothecary shop on the corner and hurried in that direction.

At the sound of the tinkling doorbell the chemist looked up from his scales and recognized his neighbor. He wiped his hands on his apron and came forward.

"Ah, Mr. Wheatley—these be bad times!" he said sympathetically.

"My letter—I wanted to read my letter. It's too dark outside. I—" Mr. Wheatley's words were almost incoherent but the chemist pushed the oil lamp forward.

"Greetings, my dear husband," ran the short letter. "Lima has suddenly taken ill. Let us bow humbly before this visitation and complain not. Go you to our friend Flag and stop in his house. God keep you as He will us. Your obedient wife and friend, Susannah Wheatley."

Inside the curtained house Mary Wheatley was staring down at a dark, grim, small person.

"No, Miss Mary!" Phillis spoke as she had never spoken before. "You stay out! Us black folks will nurse Big Lima!"

The child could not have explained the reason

for this determination. But suddenly it was as if mistress and slave, teacher and pupil, had exchanged positions. Upon the black child's shoulders fell a mantle of responsibility, clothing her in strength, maturity and assurance. Phillis felt that she must protect her beloved Miss Mary from the dreadful thing that had fallen upon them. So she sent her away and in the back of the house they waged a losing struggle with death.

Phillis did not know when Big Lima died. The day before this happened Prince picked up the small, limp form in the back hall and carried her to her room in the garret. They did not attempt then to shut Mrs. Wheatley nor Mary from that upper room. Fortunately, Phillis had a light case which did not consume her body nor disfigure her face. It was weeks, however, before she regained her strength.

By the time spring came the Wheatley household had resumed normal routine with Mrs. Crumby established as housekeeper. Mrs. Crumby had been hired by Mr. Wheatley. This worthy woman had her own husband and house full of children so could not under any circumstances "sleep out." She would, however, come in each morning by sunup and stay until sundown. Mr. Wheatley assured her the able assistance of the strong and capable Prince plus whatever the experienced Aunt Sukey could do, and also the "light help" of the girl, Phillis. Mrs. Crumby's wages amounted to what would now be about three dollars a week.

Spring rains washed Boston Town clean again. People came back to their houses, threw the doors wide and let the strong salt air of the sea blow out cobwebs and dust. Trees shook themselves, lifted their boughs to refreshing showers and soon a delicate web of green covered their nakedness. And then the asters were in bloom. By the time they could sit out under the trellis Mary and Phillis were unusually busy.

"Don't crowd the child," warned Mrs. Wheatley.

"Your eyes don't hurt, do they, dear?" asked Mary anxiously.

"Oh, no, ma'am. I feel fine." Phillis looked up from her bench. Then gathering several sheets of paper she said, "I've finished my composition, Miss Mary."

"Good! I expect Mrs. Crumby is ready for you to set the table. Run along."

Phillis hummed while she laid out the knives and forks. Mrs. Crumby peeped out from the pantry and shook her head. She couldn't make up her mind about this black child who "talked like a real lady" and read books. Funny business!

Out in the garden Mary was looking over the sheets left behind by Phillis.

"You know Nat wants to start her on Latin this summer," she explained to her mother, "so I'm

43

trying to get her well up on English. Nat will be quite put out if she's weak there."

Mrs. Wheatley turned her crochet loop and regarded the pattern intently.

"Have you finished your dress for the Winslow party, dear?" she asked.

"Not quite," Mary answered absently. "Listen to this, Mother. Really Phillis writes very well." She read:

"Today I saw the morning-glories wake. Of all the flowers in the garden they are my dearest. For they are children of the sun. When the sun goes away they bow their heads and go to sleep. What else can they do when the sun is gone? The world is dark and they cannot see. So they are silent and they sleep. But when the sun comes up again they lift their heads and they smile and their faces are glad. I heard them singing in the garden this morning when they woke. They sang because the sun was up. And I sang with them."

Mary's face was glowing with pride. "Isn't that a lovely composition, Mother? Oh, I must save it to show Nat!"

Mrs. Wheatley's face was a little anxious. "Mary," she said finally, "I'm not sure you aren't carrying this thing a little too far. Phillis is a bright and well-mannered girl. You've been wonderful with her and she's learned remarkably well. Now that she speaks so well and in addition reads and writes, I'm puzzled by your insistence to go on teaching her."

"But, Mother, if she's learned so well in this short time—why she's still only a little girl—I see no reason to stop now."

"There's one thing we have neglected." Mrs. Wheatley bit off her thread.

"Neglected?" Mary could not understand.

"The child should be christened so that she'll be a Christian."

"Why she goes to church with us every Sunday," Mary protested. "She is a Christian."

"Does she know the catechism—the Articles of Faith?"

"No-o-o." Mary spoke slowly. "I've never drilled her on them. But she can learn them herself easily enough."

"You forget that this is a heathen child. Her only salvation lies in baptism." Mrs. Wheatley spoke firmly. "I'm going to see to it that she learns the catechism."

Mary looked after her mother as she rose and went into the house. The Wheatleys were Episcopalians. Mary had been christened at the altar in Christ Church but she had not been brought up on the "fire and brimstone" sermons of Cotton Mather. She was therefore surprised at her mother's calling sweet little Phillis a "heathen." She recalled the appellation of following Sunday morning as she observed Phillis in her long cotton dress and frilled bonnet slip into the corner of their pew and fold her hands in an attitude of devout attention.

Christ Church is still known for its grave beauty and the melody of its bells. All Boston churches had one bell for soberly summoning to meeting, but Christ's had a peal of eight whose sweet, clear tones could be heard across the waters by the students at Harvard College. Inside, light filtered through colored glass onto the gleaming altar and organ music rolled over bowed heads. The Wheatleys had their own rented pew. For a long time now communicants were accustomed to point out the lovely Miss Wheatley with her carefully dressed little "serving girl" who curtsied so properly when addressed.

On this Sunday after they had returned from the service and were alone Mary asked, "Phillis, what do you like best about church?"

She was a little taken aback by the child's immediate reply:

"The bells!" Phillis raised her eyes in ecstatic recollection.

Then young Nat was home and a vigorous wave of young manhood passed through the house. But while Mary adored her twin brother his friends were mere "boys" to the provocative young woman. She was always the gracious hostess but lightly evaded their courting.

Once more Mrs. Wheatley was haunted with the specter of an "old maid" daughter.

"It's because she's turned herself into a schoolteacher. We've got to put a stop to it!" Mrs. Wheatley told her husband.

So for a spell that summer while Mary rode and boated and walked with her brother's visiting friends and other young men of Boston's nice families, Phillis learned her catechism under Mrs. Wheatley's tutelage and each day read a chapter in the Bible. Before this she had often listened to the Bible being read. Now with the Book in her own hands she became enmeshed in the grand style and rolling eloquence of the Scriptures. The assigned chapter was forgotten while she pored over many thin pages.

And this particularly delighted old Aunt Sukey who now sat alone in the gathering darkness. She was almost blind but her ears were keener than ever.

"Dat yo', chile?" she would call out gleefully as Phillis' step sounded on the gravel walk.

"Yes, Aunt Sukey. I've come to read to you."

"Bless yo', honey. Read 'bout Moses. Read how Moses go to Egypt lan' an' talk right up to dat wicked old Pharaoh."

It was an old favorite. The child sat on the ground, her legs crossed under her. A few minutes later the clear, young voice could be heard in the sonorous phrases:

And the Lord spake unto Moses, Go unto Pharaoh, and say unto him, Thus saith the Lord, Let my people go, that they may serve me.

47

And if thou refuse to let them go, behold,
I will smite all thy borders with frogs.

"He! He!" cackled Aunt Sukey. "Frogs! Frogs
ovah all the land . . . frogs everywhere!"

The old woman and the child laughed together
about the frogs and then went on with their story
of liberation.

There was something forced about the gaiety of
Boston that summer. Nathaniel Wheatley was conscious of the strain. Most of the young men were
restless and argumentative; tempers were short.
While the elegant and very rich John Hancock was
the figure after which every young blade would
like to pattern himself, strange contradictions were
encountered. For while the wigs, buckles, waist-
coats and manners of "Squire Hancock" set the
fashion, the young man's taste for the company of
cankerous old Sam Adams and loudmouthed artisans caused raised eyebrows. In the face of the
talk going on in every public house and up and
down the Mall, Nat was beginning to wonder if he
were not wasting time in school. He was ready to
say that his father's business needed "new
blood."

It was therefore with some relief that young
Wheatley saw his visitors depart and midsummer
quiet settle on the house in King Street. It was
good to lie in bed undisturbed and unhurried. He
had some thinking to do.

The house was very still that July morning when Nat finally made his way downstairs. He found only Phillis on hand to give him breakfast.

"Well! Where is everybody, Phillis?" he asked.

"Prince took Miss Mary and your mother to the dressmaker's," Phillis explained, "and Mrs. Crumby's in the shed dipping candles." Then she smiled shyly. "But I will fix everything for you, sir."

Phillis was delighted with this opportunity to serve the young master. He followed her into the kitchen and watched while she went about the business with efficiency and dispatch.

"You certainly are a smart little girl," was Nat's tribute to the stack of golden-brown buckwheat cakes, rasher of crisp pork and bowl of sugared blackberries she set before him. "Now," he said as she poured out a steaming cup of coffee, "tell me about your lessons!"

The black eyes sparkled as Phillis talked. Mary had told him of her progress but Nat was amazed at her vocabulary and her interests. The child seemingly had a real thirst for knowledge. But what was her capacity? Certainly they were far from reaching that limit now. The young man regarded the animated face with renewed curiosity. It was a pretty face.

"I think we'd better start Latin at once," Nat said finally. He stood up and stretched himself

49

comfortably. "No time like the present, eh, Phillis?"

"Oh, no, sir!" But she hesitated.

"Well, what's the matter? Why not clear the table while I run upstairs for some of my old books?"

"Er—Mrs. Crumby, sir. She told me to come help her with the tallow after you had your breakfast." Phillis' large eyes regarded him soberly.

"Ah, shucks!" The young man snapped his fingers disdainfully. "Tell Mrs. Crumby I want you. That's all!" And he turned and strode out with royal disregard of upsetting household routine.

So the lessons were continued with far greater precision and vigor, for the Harvard student was an exacting taskmaster.

"No! No!" he shouted at her. And Phillis, her eyes growing bigger and bigger, would try again.

"Sum, es, est, sumus, estis, sunt."

"The future!"

"Eram, eras," began poor Phillis, only to be interrupted with a shout.

"No! Where is your mind? Pay attention!"

Phillis gulped and tears filled her eyes but she managed to get out, *"Ero, eris, erit, erimus, eritis. . . ."* She was crying.

"Well, what on earth is the matter?" Nat regarded his pupil in amazement.

"I—I—got to—pluck the chickens—for dinner. I forgot—and Mrs. Crumby—will be mad!"

"Mrs. Crumby! Mrs. Crumby!" the young man stormed. "Who is your mistress? Who is your master? I'll speak to Mrs. Crumby myself."

"I think, Nat," interposed Mary gently, "you are pushing Phillis too hard."

"I am not," snapped Nat. "Phillis, have you memorized those lines from Pope?"

"No, sir, not yet, sir."

"Have them for me in the morning!"

So matters went for the remainder of the summer. One lovely September morning when just a hint of fall blew across the garden Mrs. Wheatley, sewing in her room, heard the clump of Mrs. Crumby's heavy feet on the staircase, accompanied by the wheeze which indicated a ruffled spirit.

"I wonder what's wrong now," Mrs. Wheatley murmured to herself. Then she called out, "Here I am, Mrs. Crumby!"

Mrs. Crumby planted herself in the doorway, hands on ample hips.

"Hit's that Phillis again. I sets her cleaning the parlor and she's in there talking to the chairs. Loafing—that's all she does."

"Oh, dear!" Mrs. Wheatley sighed and laid aside the dress piece. "All right, Mrs. Crumby, I'll go right down."

"Mumbling to herself," she continued. "Pixied—that's what she is!" The good woman offered her own solution as she went wheezing down the stairs.

"What is it, Mother," Mary called from her room, then joined her mother in the hallway. "Oh, it's Mrs. Crumby!"

"You see, Mary! Phillis is quite big enough now to work properly. You and Nat have spoiled her."

"Oh, Mother, you know Mrs. Crumby's an old scold! Phillis has to go over her lessons while she works. You should see the things Nat piles on her."

"Well, he'll be leaving this week and Phillis is going to spend more time in the kitchen."

"Mother, you can't! I—"

"Your father and I have decided that you are overdoing this lesson business. You've passed the limit of common sense and I'm putting a stop to it right now."

"I'll go with you." Mary spoke sorrowfully as they started down the broad staircase.

"It's our fault, of course, but for her own good Phillis must know that her work comes first."

"What *is* her work?" Mary asked the question softly but there was a note of rebellion in her voice.

They could hear a muffled voice now behind the thick parlor doors.

"She's probably reading something aloud," Mary whispered. "Wait! Let's crack the door a little and listen."

The oiled handle turned without a sound and then they could hear Phillis' voice. She was enunciating beautifully and with deep feeling. They stood in the hall and listened:

> The heavens declare the glory of God;
> And the firmament sheweth his handywork.
> Day unto day uttereth speech,
> And night unto night sheweth knowledge.
> There is no speech nor language, where
>   their voice is not heard.

Mary carefully closed the door and looked at her mother. Mrs. Wheatley's eyes were filled with tears. They walked away from the door.

"You see, Mother," said Mary, "she's only memorizing her Psalm for the coming Sabbath. Phillis has a *mind*. We mustn't let it wither away in darkness."

"Yes—yes—you're right." Susannah Wheatley was a good woman. She was an honest woman. Now from the depth of her goodness and honesty she grappled with a question. "But what," she asked, "can a black child *do* with a mind?"

CHAPTER FIVE

Phillis Begins to Write

The years from 1765 to 1770 smoldered and piled in Boston until a blazing bonfire burst into flame. Yet to the dark girl in the big house in King Street they were natural years of growing. Some events stood out. As a rule, however, not for the reasons later noted in history books.

There was the Sunday night in May, 1766, when all the bells began to ring. Phillis heard them in her sleep and sprang up, thinking it was Sunday morning, but her garret room was dark and when she peeped through the gable window she could see nothing outside. The bells were ringing louder and louder. Then she heard the sound of cannon coming from the direction of Castle Island and what seemed like an answering salute from some ship in the harbor.

At this she hurried downstairs and joined the others. Mr. Wheatley unlatched the door and they went out onto the porch. In other houses lights were now showing and people were calling out to know what the clamor was all about. They heard the fife and drum long before the musicians turned into their street and they could hear loud cheering in the distance. At last they could distinguish the crier's words: "Stamp Act is repealed! Rejoice! The Stamp Act is repealed! Long live the king!"

The shout went the length and breadth of the street: "Long live the king!"

"What does it mean, Miss Mary?" asked Phillis as soon as they were in the house again.

Struggling a little, Mary tried to explain. "Bad men in Parliament," she said, "had unjustly taxed the colonists, but the good king had intervened and now the tax was done away with."

Phillis listened avidly to all the talk going on. That evening they joined their neighbors carrying lighted lanterns to hang on the Liberty Tree— tallest elm in a row of ancient trees. The little girl carried her lantern and she sang and shouted along with everyone. From all sides of the Commons came men, women and children, like swarms of fireflies in the darkness. They hung the lanterns so thick on the tree that it was like a huge torch. Phillis' voice died in her throat as she looked. Never could she have pictured anything so beautiful! And all around her the people were saying, "King George is good! Long live the king!"

She saw the great lighted tree all through the night and she dreamed that the good King George came riding on a cloud and looked down on the tree. For the next few days nobody talked about anything else, but Phillis slipped off to herself and wrote a poem. She had been trying to find lines that fitted the occasion and before she realized it she was putting words together. She crossed out many words and rewrote many lines, but at last she copied what she had on a clean sheet and speaking very softly, read it aloud:

> Your subjects hope, dread Sire,
> The crown upon your brow may flourish long,
> And that your arm may in your God be strong!
> O, may your sceptre numerous nations sway
> And all with love and readiness obey.
> But how shall we the British King reward?
> Rule thou in peace, our father, and our lord!
> May the remembrance of thy favors past
> The meanest peasant most admire the last.
> May George, beloved by all the nations round,
> Live with heaven's choicest blessings crowned.
> Great God, direct and guard him high
> And from his head let every evil fly.
> And may each clime with equal gladness see
> A monarch's smile can set his subjects free!

"What have you got there, Phillis?" The child gave a start. She had been so absorbed that she had not heard footsteps on the attic stairs. Now confronted by Miss Mary she was embarrassed.

"A—it's—" she smiled shyly and handed over the sheet.

Mary was quiet for so long that Phillis thought she was displeased. But when she dared to look up, Mary dropped on her knees beside the child and put her arm about her. Then taking one of the dark hands in her own she said very earnestly, "Phillis, I want you to make me a promise."

"Yes, Miss Mary."

"Whenever you have a lovely thought—write it down. You know the beautiful poems of Horace and Pope, so you know you have written a poem. It's a good poem, too. We'll read more poetry. But I want you to take time to write down thoughts out of which you can make poetry. Promise?"

"I promise, Miss Mary."

The storm which broke about a year later in the house on King Street shook the Wheatley household more profoundly than the passage of the Townshend Acts. Nathaniel's announcement that he was *not* going to graduate from Harvard College and *not* going to be a clergyman infuriated his father and humiliated his mother. Mr. Wheatley had a great deal to say about the opportunities the "young scamp" was throwing away and his mother wept bitterly because "evil associates" had "lured" her son from the path of rectitude and virtue. Having been reared a Congregationalist, Mrs.

Wheatley blamed the whole thing on the "loose irresponsibility" of Episcopalians. Mr. Wheatley, stung by this slur upon his family's church, remarked that children usually learned obedience and reverence at their mother's knee. Torn between defense of her beloved brother and distress at her parents' pain, Mary was pale and distraught. While Phillis, hearing everything and unable to say a word, racked her brains trying to think of something she could do. She finally decided to write Nat a letter.

Upon more than one occasion the young man had instructed her to send him some item so she knew how to address him; but having made up her mind to write, she sat far into the night trying to think what to say. She could not but think that his parents were right. She had regarded every Harvard student who came to the house as a specially blessed favorite of the gods. She could not conceive how any young man could find any happier pursuit. Yet, she could not sit down and write such a letter to her young master. For several days she pondered over the matter. Gradually the solution came. After several hours of work she had a poem ready for the Harvard student. It would not be necessary to sign her name. So she simply folded and sealed the sheet and addressed it.

Nathaniel thought the handwriting was familiar before he broke the seal. By the time he had read a couple of lines he knew the missive was from Phillis.

While an intrinsic ardor prompts to write,
The Muses promise to assist my pen.
'Twas not long since I left my native shore,
The land of terrors, and Egyptian gloom:
Father of mercy, 'twas Thy gracious hand
Brought me in safety from those dark abodes.

    Students, to you 'tis given to scan the heights
Above, to traverse the ethereal space,
And mark the systems of revolving worlds.
Still more, ye sons of science, ye receive
The blissful news by messengers from heaven
How Jesus' blood for your redemption flows.
What matchless mercy in the Son of God!

    Improve your privileges while they stay,
Ye pupils, and each hour redeem, that bears
Or good or bad report of you to heaven.
Let sin, that baneful evil to the soul,
By you be shunned, nor once remit your guard;
Suppress the deadly serpent in its egg.
Ye blooming plants of human race divine,
An Ethiop tells you 'tis your greatest foe;
Its transient sweetness turns to endless pain,
And in immense perdition sinks the soul.

"Well, I'll be blessed!" The young man stared at the sheet as if he expected the words to disappear. An impulse to laugh died in the thought. Phillis' black, thin little face rose before him. It was always serious, but this—

He showed it to some of his friends. They were impressed and asked, "I say, who is the Muse?"

But Nat couldn't bring himself to tell them that

59

it was written by a little African his mother had brought home on a leash.

It was inevitable that the unusual slave girl should arouse some talk. Visitors to Christ Church always asked questions; Mrs. Crumby had her say, friends of the Wheatleys' commented and advised. It wasn't until Mrs. Leonard Wesley, one of Mrs. Wheatley's closest friends, lost her husband that people learned that the black girl wrote poetry.

Dr. and Mrs. Wesley frequently visited the Wheatleys and Phillis had been taken to their home on many occasions. When after a short illness the physician suddenly died, Phillis found herself in the midst of mourning. She wrote her poem during the night, arose very early and delivered it herself, asking the servant to take it up with the widow's breakfast tray.

The lady was profoundly moved. She could not say enough in gratitude and praise of "Mrs. Wheatley's Phillis."

There was a good deal of fighting in the streets and down on the wharves during these months. Black Prince came home one night and announced in the kitchen that he was a "son o' Libery." Mrs. Martin, the current housekeeper, snorted her disgust, but Aunt Sukey, still smoking beside the fire, demanded that he explain what he meant. His explanation may have been a bit garbled but it pleased the old lady mightily, who continued to cackle to herself all through the evening.

Business had improved after the Stamp Act was repealed; and with the arrival of the British troops "to keep order," there was more disorder but brisk trading. Mr. Wheatley allowed Nathaniel to spend some time at the shop.

On a bright fall day when the maple leaves were just beginning to turn, two gentlemen stopped in King Street to call on Mrs. Susannah Wheatley. One was the rather shabby, raw cleric just arrived in the city to pastor Second Church. He was going to pay his respects to the friend of his mother's whom he had met when a theological student. With the young clergyman was the pastor of one of Boston's large churches, a fluent, portly personage. The elder right reverend was very glad thus to shepherd his "young brother" since for some time now he had been anxious to speak to Mrs. Wheatley concerning a matter of community interest. The new pastor wished the "elder brother" had chosen another afternoon.

When, responding to their knock, the housekeeper told them Mrs. Wheatley was not at home the young man suddenly remembered a daughter and sent his name in to her.

Mary had Phillis with her in the small sitting room overlooking the garden.

"Reverend John Lathrop?" She couldn't place the name.

"He say," informed Mrs. Martin, "he was here long time ago with his ma."

"Oh, well show them in. If they came to see Mother they won't stay long."

"May I take the books upstairs and finish this?" Phillis indicated one volume.

"Of course." She looked up as a portly figure filled the doorway, and extended her hand. "How do you do, sir? Won't you come in?"

"Your most humble servant, Miss." The gentleman bowed as well as his extreme girth would permit. "Are we interrupting?"

"Indeed not. And this is Reverend Lathrop." She beamed on that gangling unfortunate, who up to that minute had been vainly trying to swallow his Adam's apple. He had recalled a leggy, thin girl with braids. The glorious creature who confronted him rendered him speechless. The men were blocking the doorway so that Phillis, holding several books in her arms, stood to one side waiting to get by. Mary now motioned toward seats but the large man boomed out:

"What have we here? This must be the young African I've been hearing so much about."

Mary flushed slightly but she turned to Phillis and said, "This is Reverend Lathrop and the Right Reverend . . ." she murmured the name.

"How do you do, sirs." Phillis spoke primly with a little curtsy.

"Quite a lady," the large man commented without moving.

Mary spoke with forced gaiety. "I'm quite willing to match Phillis with any young ladies' seminary pupil in New England!" She moved toward the window, the young man following her.

"I heard this, but I did not give it credence." There was an unpleasant edge in the other man's voice.

Phillis took a step toward the door, looked around and said, "You will excuse me, please."

"What have you there, girl?" The eyes bored down upon her.

"My books, sir."

"Let me see them."

Phillis turned her eyes toward Mary who spoke gently, "Show the reverend your books, Phillis."

"Yes, ma'am."

He took them one by one, reading the titles aloud. *"Advancement of Learning, Paradise Lost, Alexander Pope, Virgil!"* His eyes popped. "You read *Latin?*"

"Master Nat is teaching me." Phillis spoke with assurance. "I am not yet very good."

From where she was standing beside the window Mary laughed aloud.

"My brother says she shows more aptitude for the classics than I ever did!"

The gentleman turned shocked eyes on Mary Wheatley and exclaimed:

"Miss Wheatley!" Then turning abruptly to Phillis he said gruffly, "Leave us, girl!"

Phillis went out, softly closing the door behind her, but Mary stood erect, her eyes flashing, waiting for an explanation. John Lathrop stood near her, nervously biting his lips.

"Miss Wheatley—this is what I came here to talk to your mother about." The large man strode forward.

"Then," Mary spoke coldly, "perhaps you had better await my mother's return."

"But I must speak out now. You know I hold you and your dear mother in the highest esteem. Yet in this I must say you have been guilty— unwittingly, of course, of great error."

"I don't understand."

"Elder," interposed the younger man, "I think I'll be—I'll—"

"Don't interrupt me!" snapped the elder. He turned again toward the young woman and assumed a soothing manner.

"God's kind providence brought this child of Ham from the wilds of Africa to your hands that you might lead her from darkness to light, that her lost soul might be redeemed."

"Oh, she's a devout Christian." Mary spoke eagerly.

"She does not walk humbly before God and man as befits her station." The pastor gave a slight snort. "Latin! The very idea!"

"She is always gentle and obedient," Mary insisted. "But," she went on, "Phillis is very smart. My brother says that. . . ."

The gentleman waved his hand. "Really, Miss

64

Wheatley! You do your servant sad injustice. It's cruel to tax her small brain in this fashion."

"Reverend, we don't drive Phillis to books. She enjoys reading. She loves words. It's almost as if she plays with them." Mary was trying to keep her annoyance in check. She wondered how long this must go on.

"It's all imitation," the portly one was saying. "Her brain was not fashioned for creative thought."

Mary walked to the table. "Here's a sample of her own creation—her very own."

"What is it?" The reverend was suspicious.

"It's a poem." Mary tried to keep a certain snap out of her voice.

"You ask me to believe that . . . that . . . African . . . has written a poem?"

"Um-um." Mary was smiling now. And she detected something like a smile on the young man's face. She spoke to *him*. "Listen. I'll read it to you—

> Now, see the sons of vegetation rise,
> And spread their leafy banners to the skies.
> All-wise, Almighty Providence we trace
> In trees, and plants, and all the flowery race,
> As clear as in the nobler frame of man
> All lovely copies of the Maker's plan.

There you are!"

The face of the larger gentleman was flushed.

He cleared his throat and said, "Naturally she copied it some place. She couldn't have written it."

Mary opened her mouth to say something and then closed it abruptly. In the awkward silence came the young man's uncertain voice.

"My mother brought me here on a visit many years ago. I was. . . ."

"Come, Lathrop, since Mistress Wheatley is not here we need no longer intrude on the young lady." The big man was at the door.

"I'll tell my mother you were here." Mary spoke graciously. "Good day, sir."

"If you don't mind I'd like to wait. I have a note to your mother." John Lathrop wished to disassociate himself from his worthy colleague. He didn't know whether young Africans should or should not be taught Latin, but he liked the way this beautiful girl defended her charge, he liked the way her eyes flashed, he liked her spirit. In fact, the Reverend John Lathrop's heart was all aglow. He liked the girl!

When the door closed behind the irate caller they looked at each other and smiled.

CHAPTER SIX

A Summer at Newport

The house in King Street was all aflutter. There was much coming and going, delivery of packages and sending Prince on hurried errands. There was the sound of clipping shears and mumbled warnings to "Stand still!" Chairs and sofas were strewn with lengths of silk and crisp, white cotton, while streamers of ribbon curled on the rug.

The ladies were going to Newport for the season!

Mary had grown more beautiful in the past months. This trip to the most fashionable summer resort on the Atlantic seaboard was not her idea.

Now that her daughter was "receiving court" Mrs. Wheatley exhibited a strangely feminine perverseness. She thought well of Elizabeth Lathrop's son but she did not intend that he should be without rivals. A season at Newport would introduce Mary to society such as she had never known. Mary would have preferred remaining in Boston for the summer but she did not voice this preference. John had not yet "spoken."

They were taking Phillis. Though she tried to conduct herself with the modesty befitting the "serving girl" of Mistress Wheatley she could not help talking a bit to the neighbors and shopkeepers when they sent her on an errand to match a ribbon or buy thread.

"Yes, ma'am," she would say primly, *"we're* leaving, come Wednesday next," or "Indeed, ma'am, I'm certain the sea air will do my mistress good—Oh, you haven't heard? We're going to Newport!"

Phillis was slight for her estimated fifteen years. Her new dress was as long as Miss Mary's but hung straight, without supporting pads and ruffles which bellowed about Miss Mary's feet in undulating waves. Her plain little bonnet had new ribbons and the kerchief folded about her neck was crisply white. While Prince was packing their luggage in the carriage Phillis ran out to tell Aunt Sukey goodby.

The old lady ran her hand over the stiff dress stuff and fingered the new ribbons. Then she let her hand linger a moment on the girl's smooth face. It was a "pleasin'" face and Aunt Sukey could picture the shining, bright eyes.

"Walk 'umble!" Phillis had to lean forward to catch the words.

"I will, Aunt Sukey," she answered.

Aunt Sukey was so still that Phillis thought she had dropped off to sleep, but when she turned to tiptoe away the bony hand once more clutched her dress.

" 'Member—" the old lady's voice rustled in her throat.

"Yes, Aunt Sukey?"

"Da lil Jesus died for you—too," the whisper concluded. She turned her face to the wall then and closed her sightless eyes, but she was not asleep. Not until the girl had gone did she let a deep sigh escape her. Aunt Sukey knew her days were over. What there had been of hardship and of pain was past. But what of this girl with the wide-set eyes and sweet, full mouth? The old woman groaned in her feebleness. She had given the girl the best she knew.

Phillis rode on the high front seat with Prince. He glanced down at the slender, straight figure and grinned to himself.

"Um! Um!" Prince snapped the reins smartly as he spoke. "Mighty fine! Mighty fine!"

They boarded the evening packet for Newport amid much confusion, handkerchief waving, shouting and bell ringing. At the last minute Mrs. Wheatley turned tearful.

"Now, now, Mother!" Mr. Wheatley patted her shoulder reassuringly. "Everything is all right. You need a vacation."

Mary was holding a box of sweets the Reverend Lathrop had brought to the house that morning. Surrounded by chattering young friends her eyes were dreamy and she smiled serenely. Phillis clutched the ladies' parasols, veils, pillows and a small receptacle containing, among other feminine necessities, smelling salts. As soon as the boat put off they retired to the ladies' cabin. Hardly had they passed through the channel before Mrs. Wheatley was seasick. Phillis assumed the role of nurse for the night.

But she was on the deck and saw the sun come up out of the sea the next morning. She saw the gray of the sky suffused with coral pink and clouds light up with silver; she saw a green sea splashed with gold and crested with jeweled waves. Mary joined her at the rail as the boat headed inland.

Newport rose from the water in green terraces topped with bare, rocky crags and fringed about by broad, white beaches. Many-colored pavilions dotted the hillsides and here and there a tower rose out of the trees. Beyond the central grouping of buildings were gardens and orchards and on broad meadows sheep were grazing. Fishermen, bringing in their night catch, waved at them from small crafts and a big boat just ahead fluttered its sails in gay salute.

It was a gay season at Newport, that summer of 1770—the last gay season for many years. Afterward Phillis recalled her young mistress' good spirits and light laughter and was glad. The young people who sported at Newport that summer never gathered again. When the British took possession of the island, fishermen and herdsmen fled to the mainland and the soldiers slew the sheep and cut down the fine old trees for timber.

Phillis had a very special reason for remembering Newport. It was here she found Obour Tanner.

One late afternoon when the ladies were well occupied and would not need her attention, Phillis walked up the hill to get a close look at one of the town's curiosities. It was called "The Mill" and was a circular wall about ten feet in diameter and fifteen feet in height, put together without mortar and said to have been built by the Indians. As Phillis walked through the tavern gardens she saw one of the maid servants seated on a bench staring at her intently. She was a black, rather young woman, neatly dressed, evidently accompanying her mistress who, like the Wheatleys, was probably a guest in the tavern. Phillis did not like being stared at but the expression on the woman's face had something in it that made her hesitate and then smile. At that the woman said something.

Phillis never knew what it was she said. Obour

Tanner would never explain nor even speak about it again. Phillis only knew that at the sound of the woman's voice something deep inside her responded; she ran forward and then, with a puzzled look on her face, stopped.

"What did you say?" she asked.

The young woman came closer and peered into the girl's face.

"Yes," she said after a moment, "it be same. Yo' come on big ship—yo' small—like dat." With outstretched hand she indicated the height of a small child. Phillis could only nod her head. They had told her about the ship though nothing was clear in her own mind, but something was beating upon the floor of her memory now—something that made her heart race. "I come same ship," the dry voice concluded.

"What did you *say?*" The girl repeated her question, intent on this one thing. She studied the bony face with its deep hollows and ridges.

The dark woman looked away, then laid her hand on the girl's arm.

"Yo' look good—be fine dress. You got good Christian mistress, yes?" The grimace on her face was intended for a smile.

Phillis' breathing was easier. Memory was receding.

"Oh, yes," she said, almost with her accustomed brightness. "I have a sweet mistress. And you?" she asked. "Are you also blessed by God's providence?"

72

The young woman was listening to Phillis' speech with interest. Now she asked, "Yo' can read—maybe?"

"Yes." Phillis did not want to boast, so she said no more on that subject. Instead she extended an invitation. "Can you walk with me? I'm going up the hill."

This was the beginning of a friendship broken only by Phillis' death. There was always more to it than they put into words. *They had come to America on the same slave ship:* Obour was very positive on this point, but beyond that she would never go. The first time Phillis saw the long, jagged scar that reached from the woman's shoulder all the way down one arm, she cried out and exclaimed, "What a pity! How did it happen?" And Obour said quietly, "Hit's good yo' forget."

Obour belonged to a merchant's family whose place was on the hills outside Newport. During the season they often came down to the beaches and since Obour cared for the two small children she and Phillis saw a great deal of each other that summer. Obour also could read. Now she promised to "take up" writing with the help of one of the Tanner boys.

"I wanna know how hit goes with you," she told Phillis soberly when the Wheatleys were about to depart. So they promised to write each other from time to time. Obour kept Phillis' letters. Years after the young poet's death the thin packet of letters found its way into the archives of the Massachusetts Historical Society.

Meanwhile the weeks in Boston were passing tumultuously. That spring British soldiers fired into a group of colonists on the street, killing three of them instantly and wounding two others so badly that they later died. Only the intervention of cool heads and the immediate arrest of the soldiers prevented a frightful riot. All the townspeople were aroused to action. Paul Revere made an engraving for a pamphlet to sell on the street, "A Print containing a Representation of the late horrid Massacre in King Street," and on every side new groups of "Liberty Boys" were formed. Black Prince assumed a new importance in the eyes of his associates. Crispus Attucks, whom Paul Revere and the Boston selectmen honored as having been the first colonist to die in their struggle with the British soldiers, had been a friend of Prince's.

And that summer Aunt Sukey died.

The Reverend John Lathrop was so happy to welcome Mary home that he was carried away into speaking the one thought uppermost in his mind. Mary said "Yes" with charming simplicity so that King Street, which had witnessed violence, death and sadness, now became a lovers' lane.

They would have preferred a quiet wedding, but the pastor of a large church could not ignore his parishioners nor would Mrs. Wheatley be cheated. A round of Christmas gaieties was climaxed on the evening of January 31, 1771, with a wedding in the big house on King Street. The sleigh bells added their music to the night as the guests arrived and the blazing candles in every room reflected on the snow outside.

Phillis moved through the rooms quietly murmuring greetings, taking wraps, serving the guests. After the ceremony, when the cake had been cut and the lovely bride had thrown back her veil, Mrs. Wheatley lifted her hand and said, "Our Phillis has written a poem for this happy occasion. Now, if you please, ladies and gentlemen, she will recite it for you."

There was a light patter of hands and much craning of necks as the dark girl came from her place behind the serving table and stood beside her mistress. She looked around a moment and then began to speak:

Arise, my soul, on wings enraptured, rise
To praise the monarch of the earth and skies,
Whose goodness and beneficence appear
As round its center moves the rolling year.
Or, when the morning glows with rosy charms,
Or, the sun slumbers in the ocean's arms
Of light divine be a rich portion lent
To guide my soul, and favour my intent.
Celestial muse, my arduous flight sustain,
And raise my mind to a seraphic strain!

Here was the symbolism, flowery metaphors with frequent allusions to Greek mythology which made up the best classic style of eighteenth-century poetry. The guests were delighted and Phillis' sweet, musical voice and deep-set eyes held them entranced.

> Hail smiling morn, that from the Orient main
> Ascending dost adorn the heavenly plain!
> So rich, so various are thy beauteous dyes
> That spread through all the circuit of the skies,
> That, full of thee, my soul in rapture soars,
> And thy great God, the cause of all adores.

For nearly twenty minutes Phillis declaimed her lines. Finally closing with:

> Infinite Love where'er we turn our eyes,
> To Him, whose works arrayed with mercy shine,
> What songs should rise, how constant, how divine!

She bowed amid enthusiastic applause. "How sweet!" "She's a genius!" "A black poetess!"

Phillis went to the glowing bride and took her hand.

"I'm so proud of you, sweet Phillis!" These were the words she waited to hear. When she laid the white hand against her cheek it came away wet with tears.

II

THE SECOND STANZA

For bright Aurora now demands my song
Aurora, hail, and all the gathering throng!
HYMN TO THE MORNING

CHAPTER SEVEN

Phillis Defends Her Poetry

It was getting to be a polite custom in Boston to have "Mrs. Wheatley's Phillis" in to read poetry. The tempo of life moved at high speed for the men who, after twelve hours' work, had recourse to clubs and social gatherings of all description. From the richest merchant to the poorest porter, each man had one or two favorite taverns where he was more apt to be found when not working than in his own home. But respectable women had few diversions. A lady hesitated even to go to meeting unattended, though the church was the hub of her meager social life. There were no theaters and visiting troupes of players were not encouraged to remain long in the Puritan town. Since the girls' education was limited to household matters, few of the books which came from England were read by women.

Phillis, therefore, was regarded not only as an intriguing curiosity but as one whose highly gifted mind had been well cultivated. Her modest demeanor, soft voice and deep piety increased her worth in the eyes of Boston matrons and the Wheatleys were delighted to see their "prodigy" invited into the most aristocratic homes. For some time Phillis had been signing her name "Phillis Wheatley." Gradually other people referred to her in this manner so that a newcomer would have thought her a ward of the merchant's family. And now that the pastor of Second Church and his wife, Mary, had their own home in Middle Street, Phillis met the wives of other ministers and became popular among the Congregationalists. She had been baptized some time before. When she was eighteen years old she joined the Old South Church.

But Mrs. Wheatley and Mary were concerned about Phillis' health. She was delicate and her eyes were too bright.

"She's a genius!" Friends offered this as an explanation. They said that Phillis was "the spiritual type," that she was perhaps "too good for this world."

"Indeed, she is too good!" The young Mistress Lathrop was spending the afternoon with her mother. She made the comment upon being informed that Phillis had walked all the way across town to take a poem to the Reverend Mr. Pitkin, who had just lost his wife. "Everybody in town wants her to write for them. And she wears herself out weaving beautiful thoughts to give away."

Mary stood looking down into the garden. Mrs. Wheatley thought her daughter looked remarkably well in her frilled blue bonnet and she smiled indulgently. Elizabeth Lathrop's son was proving himself to be a good husband. She had not lost her daughter and yet, Mrs. Wheatley thought gratefully, how empty the house would have been without Phillis! She spoke fondly.

"Phillis calls them her 'messages of hope' and she loves to write them."

"Yes, I know, Mother, but. . . . Here she comes now!" Mary watched the dark girl hurrying toward the house.

Phillis was thin. When she reached the gate Mary saw her stop and lean against the post as though she were tired.

"Mother?" asked Mary abruptly, "has Phillis' cough gone?"

"Not altogether, I'm afraid, dear. Now that warm weather has come it is certainly better."

Two hours later the young Mrs. Lathrop walked home. She was in deep thought. In her bag was a roll of sheets. Phillis had been pleased when she asked for them.

"I always make copies for you, Miss Mary," she

said smiling. Mary was surprised at the number of sheets. The girl had written a book!

That thought kept coming back through the night. In the morning Mrs. Lathrop came to a decision. She would say nothing to John about it—yet.

Several days later a determined young matron called on the leading publisher in Boston. Publishers were also printers in those days and almanacs and pamphlets were their "best sellers." But Mary Lathrop had come to interest them in a volume of *poetry!*

"Mrs. Lathrop?" The publisher frowned at his copy boy. "What does she want?"

"She wants you to look at these!" The boy handed him half a dozen sheets of paper, then added, "She's a pippin!"

The publisher appeared not to have heard the comment but he pulled himself up and waddled to the front of the shop. His greeting was genial.

"Aha! What have we here? A poetess! Be seated, madam. How very nice." He beamed at Mary.

"I should like to have them published. They are very good." Mary felt a wave of confidence.

"Of course—of course." The publisher cleared his throat. "Let's see what you have." Looking down at a sheet he read aloud:

When from the camp of the Philistine foes,
Dreadful to view, a mighty warrior rose;

In the dire deeds of bleeding battle skilled,
The monster stalks a terror of the field.

"I say! What *is* this?"

"Oh," explained Mary, "that's from the 'Ode on Goliath.' It's quite a long piece. I didn't bring the entire poem."

"I must say this is unusual. We get all our writings from London, you know." He mumbled half aloud, reading:

And may each clime with equal gladness see
A monarch's smile can set his subjects free!

"That," interrupted Mary, "was written to the king when he repealed the Stamp Act."

The man stared at her. "Why, young woman, do you choose such extraordinary subjects for your poems? These ideas are entirely unsuited for one so—er—charming."

"Sir, you misunderstand. I didn't write those poems."

The publisher stiffened. "Madam," he said, "what trick is this? Who has sent you to me?"

It was Mary Lathrop's turn to be indignant. "No one sent me. I didn't say I wrote the poems. They were written by my mother's girl, Phillis."

"I don't understand."

Mary spoke patiently. "You see, Mother bought Phillis when she was a little girl and we educated her."

The publisher nodded. "Indeed—a bond servant!" He looked down at the sheets again. "Why, this is remarkable. I'm sorry I—"

"No, sir," interrupted the young matron. "Not a bond servant—a slave."

"What?" The man scowled. "You don't mean a—an—African?"

"Yes," said Mary, "Phillis came from Africa."

The publisher slammed down the sheets and stood up.

"Madam," he said sourly, "if you were a man— I'd—I'd—Of all the tomfoolery! This is a business house! We have no time for jokes!"

"But, sir, I assure you—"

"Good day, madam! Take your poems!"

Mary was trembling. She was on her feet and spoke haughtily.

"Phillis is well known to many persons in Boston."

"Good day, madam!"

She managed to get out onto the street with her head high. It was all she could do to keep back the tears as she hurried along, biting her lips. She was glad now she hadn't told John. He must not know about that dreadful man! She had turned off into King Street before she remembered that Phillis was not at home. Then she walked more slowly, calming herself. There must be a way!

On July 19, 1772, Phillis wrote her "Dear Friend Obour—I have been in a very poor state of health all the past winter and spring and now reside in the country for the benefit of its more wholesome air."

She was on a small farm just outside Lexington where, in return for an abundance of fresh air and all the milk she could drink, she was teaching three young Metcalfs something of reading and writing. The arrangement had been suggested to Farmer Metcalf by the Reverend John Lathrop. The farmer had agreed chiefly because of his admiration for the young pastor. Dame Metcalf was uneasy when they first brought the girl. She was not used to having black people around, but in no time all awkwardness vanished and the farmer's wife was delighted. The children "took to" Phillis at once, but it was Sara Metcalf who profited most by the dark girl's brief stay in the home.

At thirty-four the wife and mother was faded and worn. She had lost half a dozen teeth, her hair had thinned. Bad sanitation, hard work and isolation was the accepted way of life for farmers' wives. In Phillis, Sara Metcalf found not only a willing pair of hands but warm companionship and a bright mind. It is very doubtful if Phillis did much "resting" during those weeks, but she had the consolation of knowing that these good people loved and appreciated her.

In Boston Mary Lathrop was welcoming her brother. Nathaniel Wheatley had proved to be a successful businessman. The firm of Wheatley and Son was flourishing. In these turbulent times Nat got along better with the English traders than did his father. Young Wheatley, of course, had entree to the "Harvard crowd"; he dropped in at the taverns visited by the dashing John Hancock and accompanied young ladies to the Governor's Mansion. On this occasion Nathaniel had just returned from a business trip to the West Indies.

After Mary had remarked her brother's ruddy tan and exclaimed over several incidents of his trip, she brought the conversation around to Phillis.

"We must do something about her, Nat!"

Nathaniel regarded his sister with some amusement. *Women did worry about such petty things!* The young man stretched his long, silk-clad legs and regarded the tips of his buckled shoes.

"What is wrong now with our gifted pupil?" he asked.

"She has no *future!*" The deep concern in Mary's voice sobered her brother. "She's nearly eighteen. What is she going to do?"

As they looked at each other the diverse interests of their present occupations slipped away. They were the twins again, merging their two selves to solve a problem. Only then did Mary tell of her visit to the publisher.

Nat's face grew white with anger. "I'll horsewhip the scurvy bumpkin!" was his first reaction.

"No, Nat," said Mary, "that wouldn't accomplish anything. What we want to do is to get Phillis' poems in print. Then she'll begin to have real recognition. She could earn her living as a free woman."

"There are other printers." Nat was still thinking of the insult to his sister.

"Let's face it, Nat. They would all give the same answer!"

"Well, for Pete's sake! Isn't Mother constantly boasting of Phillis being invited to Mrs. So-and-So's house to read her poetry. The two of them are out all the time."

"I know, but—"

"When I came home the other day Mother was lying down and Prince had taken the carriage to *fetch Phillis*. It was raining and Mother said she might get her feet wet. If that isn't the *recognized*, spoiled poetess I'd like to know what it is!"

Mary laughed. "I know, brother mine! Phillis is a pet among the ladies. But no Boston printer is going to publish her works until you *men* set your stamp of approval on her."

Nat thought a moment and then conceded the point. Boston was ruled by a powerful clique of *men* and it was extremely doubtful that any of these men had ever heard of Phillis Wheatley.

"It's true some of their wives have had her in to tea. But the men weren't at home, so how do they know that our Phillis is a genius?" Mary regarded her brother with serious eyes. "If you would talk to them—" she left the suggestion hanging in the air.

Nathaniel frowned and stood up; he walked to the window and back again without saying a word.

Boston selectmen were very busy these days. Whose interest could they enlist in their cause right now?

"John could approach some of the clergymen," offered Mary.

"Have you suggested this to him?" asked Nat.

Mary shook her head. "I was waiting until you came back."

The twins looked at each other and grinned.

The last week in August Phillis received a letter from Mary that brought her hurrying home. The letter made no mention of the plan Nathaniel and his brother-in-law were putting into action but did tell of the "great happiness" the young wife was anticipating. Phillis' eyes filled with tears. She knew many women died in childbirth so her joy for the young mistress was not unmixed with fear.

She found Mrs. Wheatley shaken with anxiety and realized that she must be the one to sustain her. The role became easy after she went to see Mary. Mrs. John Lathrop was radiant!

"Sit down, Phillis! Oh, I'm so glad to see you."

They chatted together for a while as two close friends will who have been parted. The Metcalfs had sent love and felicitations. Mary blushed and showed Phillis the drawer of tiny garments and Phillis touched them shyly and marveled at the intricate needlework. Out of the fullness of her love Mary sensed the loneliness of the gentle dark girl. She put her arms about her then and said:

"Phillis, I have something else very important to tell you. And this is about *you!*" Then she told her what they were planning.

At first Phillis could not understand. "To publish *my* poems, Miss Mary?" she asked, bewildered.

Mary nodded her head emphatically. "That's exactly what we are determined to do. But first, you must submit to an examination."

This was an unfamiliar word. The explanation made Phillis gasp.

"Miss Mary! You want me to go to the Governor's Mansion and be questioned by the selectmen? Oh, no!"

"Listen, Phillis. It won't be the council." Mary spoke soothingly. "Just some of the men who are interested in you and want to know you."

"But why, Miss Mary? Why?" Phillis asked the question a little wildly.

Then Mary told her about the publisher.

"Phillis, that man as good as called me a liar!"

"Miss Mary!" Shock robbed her of her voice.

"So this is why we want you to go before examiners and prove that you wrote the poems— prove it to everybody."

Phillis was still. Now she understood. *They*— bad people, somewhere—doubted Miss Mary's word. That meant they doubted the word of all her friends. They were taking away their good name—blackening their character. Only she, Phillis, could put an end to this calumny. She lifted her eyes.

"I'll go." She spoke softly. "I'll tell them I wrote the poems."

Mary took her cold hands in hers. "It means more than that, Phillis. But you need not worry." She smiled. "I'm sure none of their questions will be as hard as Nat's. During the next few weeks you just look over your notebooks. Mr. Oliver will let Nat know when you're to come."

Nathaniel noted the dark, thin face bent over the old books and felt a qualm of anxiety. For the most part his request had been met with tolerant amusement.

"Oh, yes," was conceded more than once. "I've heard my wife speak of your wonderful African."

Governor Thomas Hutchinson's calendar was less crowded that fall of 1772 than it had been for many a week. It seemed a propitious time to get together a few of the port's influential men on something that had nothing to do with politics—especially since the matter had been suggested to him in a very friendly manner by the unpredictable Mr. Hancock. During the latter part of September came the summons for "Miss Phillis Wheatley to present herself on the first day following the Lord's Day of the next week, promptly at ten o'clock." The late hour was a concession to Mr. Hancock who, unlike most of his fellow townsmen, was known to lie abed long after sunrise.

Of course Mary could not go. Mrs. Wheatley planned to accompany Phillis but on the appointed morning she was seized with one of her severe headaches. So a short time before the fatal hour Phillis set off in the chaise with only Prince.

Prince was well aware of the importance of the occasion and he drove in dignified silence. Phillis was trying vainly to remember *anything* she had been reading the past days. Her throat was dry and her mind seemed a blank.

When he helped her to the sidewalk Prince gave her arm a little squeeze followed by a reassuring pat on the shoulder. His wide mouth flashed into a grin.

"Pray for me, Prince," whispered the girl. "Please pray for me!"

"I'll do dat, chile," he assured her. But as he saw the black-clad slender figure disappear behind the thick doors he wished he were on more familiar terms with his Maker.

After what seemed an interminable period of waiting she was taken into a large room where around a gleaming, oval table sat a body of stern-faced men. She stood alone under the high ceiling and fear clutched at her skirts. Then she heard: "His Excellency, Governor Hutchinson!" and through the door a man came walking toward the head of the table. Her legs trembled as she curtsied.

"So, 'tis Mistress Wheatley's Phillis!" The governor's tone was kindly. "No formidable savage here, eh, Mather?" He was addressing the Reverend Samuel Mather of the already-famous family.

The Reverend Mather's tone was dry. "Comeliness and virtue are not always handmaidens." Then he called, "Come forward, girl." And when Phillis stood in the place indicated, he asked, "Who christened you?"

"The Reverend Samuel Sewall, sir."

Before the murmur of approval had subsided the command came:

"Name the Gospels."

"Matthew, Mark, Luke and John." Phillis was breathing easier now and the faces were coming into focus.

"No fault there," she heard a voice saying. "But since they say you write poetry give me the first line of Pope's *Essay on Criticism*."

"Oh, I say, Hubbard," Andrew Oliver, Massachusett's lieutenant governor, intervened, "you can't expect the girl to—"

But Phillis was already speaking: "First follow nature, and your judgment frame by her just standard, which is still the same."

"Did you hear?" the governor asked, looking around the table. "Why that was perfect."

"And what do you think of that advice?" asked Richard Carey, Esq.

"Sir, Alexander Pope is the master—I but a humble disciple."

They were leaning forward now, these men of the New World. The girl's answers were pleasing. John Irving spoke next. He was a selectman, perhaps Boston's richest real estate dealer, but he had never gone to Latin School.

"They say you've studied Latin. Give us a line."

"Delirant reges, plectuntur Achivi," said Phillis immediately. "The translation is: The monarch's folly makes the people regret."

Somebody laughed. It was a short laugh and the governor cleared his throat.

"I think, gentlemen," he said, "we may proceed directly to the matter of the poems. There are several allusions here that I should like to have explained."

She was perfectly calm now. She told them how she happened to write the "messages of hope," of her gratitude to King George for having repealed the Stamp Act. She told the story of how Niobe's children had been slain by Apollo and why she was moved to put that story into poetry.

They were nodding their heads and declaring themselves satisfied when the door abruptly opened and into the room came an elegant figure that bowed to the governor and spoke apologetically.

"Sir, I regret that I am late. I do ask your pardon."

"Tut, tut, Hancock," said the governor. "You have missed a good party. We are just about to sign our statement."

John Hancock looked around the table and his eyes came to rest on the dark girl standing at the end.

"The examination is completed?" he asked.

"And most successfully," John Moorhead spoke enthusiastically. The others nodded. The clerk at the governor's elbow was writing busily with a long quill.

John Hancock's face broke into his most charming smile.

"Then may I ask if the poetess would render one of her poems—just for me?"

They all looked in her direction and Phillis smiled shyly. She had heard of this John Hancock. Nat was given to hero worship where he was concerned. For a moment they waited and then her clear voice sounded:

Should you, my lords, while you peruse my song,
Wonder from whence my love of Freedom sprung,
Whence flow these wishes for the common good
By feeling hearts alone best understood,
I, young in life, by seeming cruel fate
Was snatched from Afric's fancy'd happy seat;
What pangs excruciating must molest,
What sorrows labour in my parent's breast!
Such, such my case. And can I then but pray
Others may never feel tyrannic sway?

After that they crowded about her and shook her hand. The paper was passed around for their signature. They all signed, assuring "the world that

94

the poems specified were, as we verily believe, written by Phillis, a young Negro girl. . . ."

John Hancock walked with her to the chaise, and he said, "You are a good American!"

Black Prince held his head very high as he drove her home.

CHAPTER EIGHT

Castles in England

Phillis Wheatley continued writing but her poems remained unpublished. Then in January, 1773, she sent a letter to her "Dear Friend" in Newport:

> How doth the Lord move in mysterious ways His wonders to perform! Little did I think that my poor lines on the death of the good Reverend Whitefield would be noted by the gracious and most generous Countess of Huntingdon. But now comes the bereaved Widow with a message from the Countess herself.

Obour, reading the letter in Newport, muttered to herself with excitement. Here was a case of good seed bearing much fruit!

George Whitefield had been one of the older Harvard students brought home by Nathaniel. The girl he married was a friend of Mary's. When the charming Countess of Huntingdon visited Boston and chose the young American clergyman to serve as chaplain in her castle on the Thames, Boston society stirred with excitement. Mary, accompanied by Phillis, was in the crowd which waved the young couple off.

The news of George Whitefield's sudden death brought sadness and dismay. With Mary's letter of condolence went a poem written by Phillis.

All this had happened months before Mary Lathrop's daughter was born and the Wheatley's world started revolving around that tiny bit of pink humanity. When Mrs. Wheatley was not at her daughter's house Phillis was on hand. Mr. Wheatley and Nathaniel might grumble about being neglected but nobody paid any attention to them.

On a clear, bright January morning when Mary was allowed to sit up for a few hours a caller was announced. It was the heavily veiled widow of George Whitefield. The young mother's shining eyes clouded with tears as she embraced her friend and Phillis slipped out of the room to leave them alone.

After a time Phillis heard Mary calling to her. She hurried to the room.

"Dear Mrs. Whitefield wants to thank you for your poem, Phillis," said her mistress.

Phillis took the visitor's extended hand and pressed it gently.

"It was so—so—kind of you." The widow's lips trembled. She was fumbling in her black reticule and finally drew out a thin packet. "The countess sends you a letter." Phillis glanced at Mary's flushed face as she took the folded paper with its stamped crest and her name written in a bold, flourishing hand. Her hands trembled as she broke the seal and unfolded the thick, yellow sheet. At first the lines danced before her eyes but in a moment she read aloud:

My dear Miss Phillis,

Your beautiful lines written on the death of our most worthy Chaplain touches us deeply. With the consent of the bereaved widow we are having them printed so that they may be framed and hang as a memorial to one whose faithful service we would always remember. We should be most happy if you could be here when this is done. Accept our thanks and a cordial invitation to come to England where your rich and bountiful gifts will find a warm welcome.

And at the bottom of the page was elegantly inscribed, "Countess of Huntingdon."

It was a miracle! A countess had published her poem—an invitation from a high lady in England! No one, least of all, Phillis, contemplated accepting the invitation. It was enough that it had come—enough that the poem had been printed. But then a number of unrelated circumstances conspired to bring about the event.

First, Nathaniel finally persuaded his father to cement good business relations with certain English merchants by opening a branch in London. Second, in spite of the signed affidavit Mary Lathrop could not persuade a single printer in Boston to publish the poems. Third, early in March Elizabeth Whitefield told her friends that she was returning to England and about that time Phillis began coughing again.

"Since Nat's going over he could take Phillis." Mary voiced her thoughts casually. "I'm sure the countess would use her influence for having the poems published."

"And the sea trip would do her good," Mrs. Wheatley spoke thoughtfully. She was worried about Phillis.

"Really, Mother," objected Nathaniel when the idea was broached to him. "I can't—"

"I'd be glad to accept responsibility for the girl," offered Mrs. Whitefield.

But when the May morning came that her son and the dark girl whom she had taken into her heart were to sail for England Mrs. Wheatley could scarcely hide her grief. A trip across the Atlantic Ocean was a long and perilous undertaking in 1773. Many ships were wrecked with all on board lost; deadly epidemics frequently broke out among the passengers or crew; mutiny was a common occurrence and murderous pirates roved the seas.

"Now, now, Mrs. Wheatley," the Widow Whitefield spoke soothingly. "Providence rules the briny deep. We are in His hands."

Black Prince was very officious as he stored their belongings on board. The *Dolly Ann* was a fine American ship, well supplied with mahogany furniture, mirrors, excellent copper stoves and even rugs. But passengers were warned to take along an extra blanket, plenty of warm clothes and as much fresh fruit as they liked. Gentlemen always checked their wines. Farewell parties on deck just before sailing were often very gay.

Just before visitors returned to shore Phillis slipped a roll into her mistress' hand.

"This is for you," she whispered shyly, "read it when you get home."

Then Mr. and Mrs. Wheatley were on the wharf surrounded by friends who waved until the ship swung into the bay and out of sight. As they drove home behind Prince Mrs. Wheatley cried softly. Mr. Wheatley patted her shoulder with masculine assurance.

Mary and the baby were waiting at home. She would have liked to have gone to the ship's sailing but could not leave her four-month-old daughter. She listened eagerly while they recounted all the details.

"What have you there, Mother?" she asked.

Mrs. Wheatley was still clutching the roll of sheets.

"Oh, I'll open it. I know it's a poem." And they unrolled the sheets on the table and read:

A Farewell to America

Adieu, New England's smiling meads,
Adieu, the flowery plain;
I leave thine op'ning charms, O spring,
And tempt the roaring main.

"Now, Mother," Mary had to warn her mother who gulped.

There were twelve stanzas, some of the lines written directly to her mistress as:

Susannah mourns, nor can I bear,
To see the crystal shower
Or mark the tender falling tear
At sad departure's hour;

Not unregarding can I see
Her soul with grief oppressed
But let no sigh, nor groans for me
Steal from her gentle breast.

"The dear child!" sighed Mrs. Wheatley.

"This will be wonderful for her," said Mary happily.

The weather was ideal. Not once were they blown out of their course and so they made the trip in the unusual short time of fifty-one days. Early in the morning of July 12th they sailed into the harbor of Liverpool. Accompanied by Nathaniel Wheatley and Mrs. George Whitefield, the dark eighteen-year-old landed in England.

They rode up to London in the stagecoach. For the first time Phillis heard the music of stage horns and the drivers' cheery "Tallyho!" The lush, dark green of gently undulating countryside filled her with a joy that seemed faintly familiar. Everything appeared to be so cozy and compact with a soft, blue sky just above the treetops.

It was evening when they alighted at the Red Cock Hostelry in Charing Cross. Before Phillis could get more than a blurred impression of many lights, loud voices and heavy smoke, the ladies were whisked away to their rooms. Nathaniel saw to it that supper was sent up to them. Then that young man disappeared for his first glimpse of London night life.

For a long time Phillis could not sleep. She lay stiff and still, listening to the rumbling of the great city; the narrow bed seemed to rise and fall, continuing the roll of her berth on the ship. Something of her old terror of the dark touched the girl and she rose quickly and lighted a candle. On the other side of the room Mrs. Whitefield lay sleeping peacefully. The sound of her regular breathing reminded the dark girl of how she once depended on Mary's nearness in the night. After a moment she blew out the candle and slipped back into bed. Somewhere outside in the city a great bell boomed the hour.

In the morning Nathaniel secured a driver to take them to the castle.

"Be a good girl, Phillis, and mind your manners!" His smile encouraged her as they took leave and started on this last lap of their journey. Phillis looked back at him until they turned the corner. A lump filled her throat. For now every dear, familiar face was gone. She was among strangers.

But the sweet sound of bells dispelled her gloom.

"It's the Westminster chimes," Mrs. Whitefield informed her. "Sometimes we can hear them all the way up the Thames."

They were driving through a square with trees and green plots and graveled walks where ladies strolled with tipped parasols and neatly dressed maids pushed baby perambulators in the sunshine.

"Where is the fog?" asked Phillis.

Mrs. Whitefield gave a tinkling laugh. "You colonials!" She spoke now like an experienced cosmopolite. "Thinking London is always in a fog! You'll see lots of sunshine in England."

They left the city behind and rolled along beside the river. Phillis could look back and see the famous old bridge under which small craft clustered. Gradually the wharves gave way to greensward that reached to the water's edge and sailboats skimmed like white birds on the surface. Then Mrs. Whitefield pointed up the hill to where a tower could be seen rising among the trees.

"There it is!" she said.

The long, slanting rays of afternoon sun lighted the ivy-covered walls and stone turrets as they approached. A high, thick hedge marked the course of an ancient moat, and the arch through which they passed into the wide driveway had once been a great gate. The air was fragrant with many blooms and in the center of the circling driveway a fountain played.

The Countess of Huntingdon was a kindly, generous woman who delighted in good works. The role of patron of the arts may have been a new one for her but the fact that the artist in this case was a young poetess from America, one of an enslaved people, added piquant excitement to the idea. She had been encouraged in the undertaking by her friend Lord Dartmouth.

"A black poetess!" Lord Dartmouth had exclaimed. "My dear countess, she will be the rage!"

They had not expected to see anyone so comely and well bred. That night after Phillis had been conducted to her room the countess, a visiting friend and Mrs. Whitefield talked until a late hour.

"What perfect manners!" exclaimed the visiting lady. "And her eyes are beautiful."

"Such small hands and feet!" The countess spoke thoughtfully. "I'm inclined to think the right clothes would set off her black skin."

"I've never seen a black person really dressed."

The American widow was rather overwhelmed by the Englishwomen's enthusiasm.

"She has a good figure," commented the countess' friend.

"The skin on her face is smooth and fine. I wonder if her neck and shoulders are equally good." The countess evidently had several things in mind.

Since servants were plentiful and cheap in England slaves were very rare. They were indeed a luxury indulged in only by a few rich or eccentric men who wanted unusual body servants or who had acquired the habit. But London sometimes entertained dark and richly clad visitors from India, from Algiers, from Ethiopia. It was well known that some of these visitors were powerful and learned as well as wealthy. In eighteenth-century England Phillis' dark skin was not looked upon as a badge of shame but rather as a novelty. So the countess dressed her protégée as she thought fitting and when everything was in order she gave a garden party to present her to the countryside.

Phillis was a success. Her modest demeanor, soft voice and charming manners won the guests and her poetry was acclaimed. In December the first edition of her poems was published for A. Bell, Bookseller in Aldgate Street. The slender volume was dedicated "To the Right Honourable the Countess of Huntingdon" by her "Very humble and devoted servant, Phillis Wheatley." As a preface was a statement by John Wheatley telling how "Phillis was brought from Africa to America in the year 1761" at a very tender age and how "by only what she was taught in the family, she, in sixteen months time from her arrival, attained the English language, to which she was before an utter stranger, to such a degree as to read any of the most difficult parts of the sacred writings, to the great astonishment of all who heard her." Also as part of the Preface was the affidavit signed by sixteen of the most prominent men in the colony of Massachusetts. The poem which was the most widely remarked was the girl's translation from Ovid's *Metamorphoses*, because in addition to translating from the Latin she had lines of her own woven into the story of Niobe's distress for her slain children. The "Black Poetess," as they called her, did become the "rage." At a big party given for her in London by Lord Dartmouth, the onetime Lord Mayor of London, Brook Watson, presented the dark girl with a Foulis edition, in folio, of *Paradise Lost*, the masterpiece of England's most lauded poet in 1773. This folio was sent to Harvard College in 1824, thirty years after Phillis Wheatley's death.

The only picture of Phillis which was widely printed in America is that of the girl seated with her quill in hand and wearing the white kerchief and fluted cap of the serving girl. But while she was in London another picture was made. She is wearing a full décolleté gown of some soft material; her full lips are smiling and her large eyes are wide. This was the picture she sent home for Christmas. Mrs. Wheatley showed it proudly, saying with motherly affection:

"See! Look at my Phillis! Does she not seem as though she would speak to me?"

Even then the good woman was far from well. But she wrote nothing of this either to Nathaniel or Phillis.

Plans were under way to present Phillis at court when the king and queen returned to St. James. And then came a letter from Mary:

"Mother is ill. She does not want to call you from the happy scenes of your triumph but we sorely need you. I am going to have another baby and my strength fails."

Phillis did not hesitate for one moment. Her family needed her. Her new friends did not try to draw her from what she clearly saw as "the path of duty." The countess deeply appreciated the girl's devotion and concern.

It was only a matter of days before Phillis was once more on the "briny deep," but this time she was alone and the passage was rough and stormy. For a while after Phillis' return her mistress seemed to improve. But sadness and grief were in store for the household. It soon became evident that Mrs. Wheatley's illness was becoming more serious. On March 3, 1774, the good Mistress Wheatley died.

CHAPTER NINE

A Poem for George Washington

Phillis wrote a heartbroken letter to Obour—"Imagine the loss of a parent, sister, and brother—the tenderness of all these were united in her. I was a poor little outcast and stranger when she took me in; not only into her house but I became a sharer in her most tender affections. I was treated by her more like her child than her servant. Do, my dear friend, remember me and this family in your prayers."

She had to be a source of strength for the family. Nathaniel was haunted by a sense of guilt because he had reached Boston only on the day of his mother's death. He bitterly reproached himself for not having left England with Phillis.

"She knew you were coming, Master Nat," Phillis comforted him.

John Wheatley walked about as though dazed and Mary in her weakened condition was prostrated.

For weeks Phillis had her hands full. Neighbors and friends were kind. They wanted to hear about London and of all the wonderful things that had come to Phillis, but the young woman had neither the time nor inclination to talk of those fairylike days. It all seemed like a beautiful dream from which she had been rudely awakened.

But she brought back her book of poems and these began to get about.

"I shall send the five books you wrote for," she says in a letter to Obour. "If you want more they shall be ready for you."

In May Nathaniel returned to London.

"Give the countess my love." For a moment Phillis saw the garden with its boxed hedges and fountains and a sigh escaped her.

Nathaniel studied the expressive, dark face. Phillis was a woman now and he had seen how London received her. Yet here she was in her straight, dark dress and apron, with the wide, sincere eyes unchanged by all the pomp and glitter she had witnessed. What did America hold for her? He took her hand in his.

"There will be more poems, Phillis," he said. "I'll send you a box of books—whatever they are reading in London now. And one of these days you'll go back."

But Phillis shook her head. "I don't think so, Master Nat. My place is here."

Then on June 1st the British closed Boston Port. Parliament took this drastic step because the people of Boston had not paid for the shipload of tea which had been dumped into the harbor the winter before. General Gage moved in with his soldiers and the town was put under military control.

The wharves were entirely deserted. There was no work and it was predicted that people would soon starve in the streets. Salem and Marblehead offered the use of their wharves to Boston merchants. At night carts carrying goods from these ports into the beleaguered town rumbled along the road.

There was no business but John Wheatley walked down to the shop every morning and returned each evening with a heavy heart. When Phillis suggested that they could let the housekeeper go he agreed with a nod of his head. Thereafter, with the help of Prince, Phillis did all the housework.

Mary Lathrop's second child, a boy, was born in August. The careworn Reverend John Lathrop tried to be briskly cheerful. But Mary was a long time recovering. The weather was very hot. Vegetable gardens shriveled for want of rain; many cows were dry. Even when milk was lowered into

110

the well to keep cool it soured before dark. In order to relieve Mary as much as possible Phillis kept the little girl with her at her grandfather's. After a while Mary was going about as usual. But all her youth had drained away.

Throughout the summer the air was filled with the roll of drums and the heavy clumping of British boots. It was impossible for Phillis to associate the stiff-jointed soldiers of General Gage whom she saw drilling on the Commons with the warm-hearted people she had met in England. All the colonies were aroused by what the British were doing to Boston. By fall Minute Men were drilling on every village green in New England.

The winter of 1774-75 was the mildest on record—which probably had much to do with General Gage's eventual defeat. For farmers, townsmen, loafers and woodsmen kept on drilling; therefore, when in April General Gage decided to cross the river and strengthen certain forts he met with very effective resistance on the roads to Lexington and Concord. After that rather bloody skirmish the British went about organizing Boston to withstand a real siege and many people fled from the city.

The Wheatleys did not go away—nor did Reverend Lathrop and his family. Second Church congregation was made up of small shopkeepers, artisans and workmen. They had no place to go and their pastor would not leave them. But the Lathrops did close their house on Middle Street and come to live in the old Wheatley house on King

Street. The Quartering Act gave British soldiers the right to be put up in any man's house. And soldiers were taking over all the fine old houses which had been deserted by their owners.

"If you don't come, Miss Mary," urged Phillis, "they'll move soldiers in on us. And that would kill your father!"

Mary knew that Phillis was thinking chiefly of her and that she was cheerfully taking on more work, but she thought longingly of the airy rooms and the garden for the children and she knew Phillis and her father were lonely.

So it was decided and the big house was no longer empty. As spring came and the garden began to bloom there was talk and cheer and some laughter in the rooms. The women worked together through the day and in the evening when the babies were asleep they sat and sewed or knitted while the men talked about the war. Frequently a visitor stopped in with the latest news.

At this time it was not known whether or not the other colonies would back New England. It might be that this war which they had started on the Lexington Road would be a private matter between Massachusetts and the entire British Empire. It was to guard against such a possibility that they had sent their most eloquent delegates to the Continental Congress meeting in Philadelphia. During the anxious weeks of waiting, white and coral fruit trees filled the air with fragrance and patches of violets hid under damp moss. Hyacinths and asters bloomed and then the climbing roses wrapped sagging fences and old sheds in beauty.

In these days Phillis chatted freely about her trip. Her accounts brought a flush of happiness to Mary Lathrop's cheek and made her eyes shine with pride. Mary had Phillis try on the lovely dresses which the countess herself had packed so carefully; she rummaged through little trinkets and laughed aloud as she read the names on cards. Mary was a girl again—and Phillis her adoring follower! John Lathrop was happy over seeing his wife looking so well and John Wheatley's lonely heart was comforted.

Black Prince had spaded up most of the yard for vegetables and he was wonderfully clever at getting other supplies from the oxcarts that managed to slip through the lines at night. But one night Prince did not return. They said nothing to Mr. Wheatley but in the morning John Lathrop went out to make discreet inquiries. He came back with no news. When Mr. Wheatley asked for Prince they had to tell him. Three days later they heard something:

"The English are offering to free all slaves who join them!"

They looked at each other but Phillis cried out, "I don't believe it! Prince wouldn't go over to them!"

Mr. Wheatley shook his head sadly. "I should have given him his freedom long ago. It's my fault!" Tears filled Phillis' eyes as she turned away.

Warm showers fell on the night of June 16th and the sun came up on a lovely day of fresh-washed roads, clean meadows and rich greens. On such a morning it is broad daylight by five o'clock and the Wheatley household was all astir by six. John Wheatley announced that he was going for a walk.

"Be careful, Father!" Mary spoke anxiously. The shop had been looted and there was really nothing to take him downtown.

But the old gentleman picked up his cane and set out. So it happened that he ran right into the teamsters with mules and cannon as they were being dragged toward the river. The streets were filled with soldiers headed in the same direction. Scarlet-coated officers shouted orders as the howitzers and heavy mortars rumbled along.

"They be fightin' 'cross the river this day!" Mr. Wheatley heard the mumbling voice at his elbow and turned his head. The speaker was a country bumpkin with ragged cap pulled low over strag-gling locks. He stood carelessly but his bright eyes were alert and John Wheatley was not afraid to speak his thoughts.

"God help our men!" he said fervently.

The fellow nodded his head. "Been throwin' up earthworks on Breed's all night," he said softly. "We be ready for 'em!" Then he was gone and John Wheatley turned back home.

It seemed like an evil dream as the sun rose higher in the heavens. But shortly before noon they heard the muted thunder of a firing cannon. They went up on the roof then and looked toward Charlestown. Came another cannon roar and then another. Then the air was shattered with a blast of shot that shook the house and would seem to rend the skies. Now smoke began to rise across the river and the women fell on their knees in prayer. The Battle of Bunker Hill had begun.

The battle went on all through the hot afternoon. The smell of powder and of burning wood filled the air. As blast after blast shook the earth they heard the scream of horses and when darkness fell they could see the flames. But it was quiet then—quiet until they heard in the streets the rumble of carts bringing back the wounded.

"No! You can't go, Miss Mary. You got to stay here with the children."

"I'm afraid for you, Phillis! They may harm you."

The two women whispered together in the lower hall. Phillis gently pushed Mary to one side.

"Let me go, Miss Mary! I'll be all right because they need my help."

Phillis Wheatley went out into the dark street. There was no need to ask directions. She knew the carts were going to the Commons where they were laying the wounded soldiers on hastily improvised cots. Phillis did what she could—fetched water and washed away dirt and grime and blood, held a lantern while the stretcher-bearers lowered their burden, made up more cots which were quickly filled. The bloodstained coats had been smart and red in the morning but now, as she cut them away, it was only the blood that Phillis saw. She heard no rejoicing or talk of who had won the battle as she went from cot to cot. She heard only groans and feeble calls for water and the curses of doctors as they leaned helpless over the ever-lengthening rows of cots. She did not find Black Prince among the wounded.

But there was rejoicing when the news spread that George Washington, Commander-in-Chief of the Continental Army, was encamped just across the river!

"Now, the redcoats will be scampering back to England!" they said.

One night Mary was awakened by a little cry from the baby and got up quickly, being careful not to waken her husband. The hall was faintly gray. Perhaps the little fellow had decided he had slept enough for one night. But he quieted and as the mother was about to slip back into her room she noticed a light showing under Phillis' door. Could she be sick? Mary listened but could hear no sound. Nevertheless she pushed open the door.

Phillis sat at her table, fully dressed and with a quill in her hand. When she glanced up startled, Mary whispered, "Phillis, you've written a new poem. I can see it in your face!"

116

Phillis nodded her head. She looked down at the sheets in front of her and then out the open window. What she saw brought a little frown.

"I—I—guess I've been writing all night." She spoke apologetically. Then she said, "It's for General Washington." Mary leaned over her shoulder and read in a low voice:

Celestial choir, enthroned in realms of light
Columbia's scenes of glorious toils I'll write;
While freedom's cause her anxious breast alarms,
She flashes dreadful in refulgent arms.
See mother Earth her offspring's fate bemoan
And nations gaze at scenes before unknown!

"Oh, Phillis! This is magnificent!" She picked up another sheet at random:

Shall I to Washington their praise recite?
Enough thou knowest them in field of fight.
Thee first in place and honours, we demand
The grace and glory of thy martial band.
Famed for thy valour, for thy virtues more,
Hear every tongue thy guardian aid implore!

"How many sheets are there? Phillis, he should see this!"

"You like it then?" A happy smile was spreading over Phillis' face. "If you think it's good I'll take it to him."

"Like it? Oh, my dear!" Mary bent and kissed the girl on her forehead. "But now do go to bed."

117

Later that day Phillis copied all the lines carefully on clean sheets of paper. She asked Mary not to say anything to the men about it.

"Master Wheatley might forbid me to go through the lines!" she exclaimed.

Mary thought this quite likely. Indeed, she hesitated in her role of accomplice for such a daring plan.

"Wouldn't it be better to send it, Phillis?" she asked.

"By whom?" Phillis asked. "Indeed, Miss Mary, I'm sure the soldiers won't bother me at all. They would stop a man."

Phillis washed and pressed the frilled white cap she seldom wore now, tied a clean apron around her waist, then with a little basket on her arm the slender, black serving maid set forth on an errand for her "master." When questioned she spoke timidly, with downcast eyes, and the soldiers hardly bothered to hear what she said. It was not until she was across the river and actually inside the Continental Army lines that she drew attention. For in this camp of Yankees the sight of a neatly dressed black serving girl was a rare novelty. There was coarse laughter and shouted comments.

"Look ye! A woman!"

"Where is your master?"

"Quiet, men, perchance she brings victuals!"

"Ah, yes, victuals!"

Phillis was looking around, somewhat dismayed, when she heard a loud command:

"Quiet, there!"

She looked up gratefully as a thin, rather young-ish man came toward her and asked in a hoarse voice, "What do you want, girl?"

"I seek General Washington, sir."

At the sound of her voice, accompanied by the little curtsy, the soldier looked hard at her. After a moment he said,

"The general is not here. I am his aide and will take the message from your master."

Phillis hesitated. The soldier's hawklike eyes were studying her. She felt her cheeks burning.

"It is—" she began. Then her words came in a rush. "I have a poem for him."

"A poem! By Gad!" The soldier slapped his thigh. "I knew I'd seen your face before. You're the Black Poetess!"

Now Phillis stared at him. Who was this man? Surely she had never seen him before.

"I saw you riding one day in a carriage." The man's ugly face was beaming.

But a sudden suspicion shot through Phillis' mind. "You are an Englishman?" she asked. And when he nodded she asked quickly, "What are you doing in *our* camp?"

The soldier's eyes twinkled. "You'll likely find me where men are fighting for freedom. The gen-eral will be honored to receive your poem, miss. And I shall ask him to let me publish it."

Phillis' eyes opened wider. "You are a print-er?"

119

The soldier spoke indifferently. "Among other things." He grinned then and added, "I scribble sometimes, too."

Phillis had taken the folded sheets from her sleeve and held them in her hand. She no longer distrusted the soldier. As she handed him the sheets she said shyly, "I should like to know your name, sir."

Then he took off his three-cornered hat and bowed low.

"My name," he said, "is Tom Paine and I am at your service."

She sighed then with relief because she was sure she had never heard the name before. It would have seemed unforgivable to forget anyone who had been kind to her in a strange land. She smiled.

"I take it, sir, we did not meet in London."

"We did not, miss." At the time she did not understand his crooked smile. "I should be happy to invite you to tea now—but we have no tea."

She smiled and said, "I would have brought you some tea—but there is none on our shelf. I bring only a poem."

He placed a seat for her in a sheltered spot that she might rest awhile. She saw his face light up while he read the lines she had written. When he told her goodby at the river's edge, the young aide said,

"It will mean much to Washington to know that he is first in your hearts."

THE STORY OF PHILLIS WHEATLEY

CHAPTER TEN

Springtime of a Nation

The stranger who knocked with his cane upon the door of the Wheatley house one February afternoon in 1776 was a colored man who stood quite straight in his short breeches and well-fitted waistcoat, in spite of lacking a long cape to protect him from the cold.

"Do I address Miss Phillis Wheatley?" He bowed and asked the question when Phillis opened the door.

For a moment Phillis could only stare. This was the most handsome man she had ever seen! His lean, clean-shaven face beneath the white wig was the color of a new penny, and he smiled with little crinkles about his eyes. In a voice which fluttered in her throat she assured him that he did address Miss Phillis Wheatley.

He bowed again and extended a thin packet. "I have the pleasure to deliver a letter from your friend Obour Tanner."

Phillis spoke eagerly then. "Please to come in," she said. "I have been much worried. Perhaps you could take my reply to her long-awaited letter."

"My name is John Peters," explained the stranger as he stepped into the hall. "I have heard much about you from Obour."

She led him through the cold passageway to the bright kitchen where a savory pot simmered on the stove. Because firewood was so scarce in Boston that winter kitchens were serving as living rooms. But this kitchen was a cheerful place with its crisp, dimity curtains and pieces of colored pottery. The children were playing on the floor near the window.

"You will excuse us, please," Phillis felt it necessary to apologize. "We have no fire in the front of the house."

He seated himself easily and said, "I understand." He smiled at the little girl who approached and showed him her rag doll, and he touched the doll admiringly while Phillis broke the seal on her letter and read. The siege had well-nigh wiped out mail service and Phillis had no idea how her friend was faring. Now she learned that Obour's family had fled from Newport and were in Worcester where Obour wrote she was doing "as well as could be hoped." The visitor appeared to take no notice of Phillis as she read. As a matter of fact no play of expression on her responsive face missed his eyes.

How fine she is! he thought to himself.

John Peters was a free Negro and proud of that fact. His origin is obscure but all accounts agree that he was a man of talents, intellectual attainments and charm. There are those who said he was "too proud to work." It may be that John Peters, along with other eighteenth-century men, had certain fixed ideas about what "gentlemen" did or did not do. But that he would not work hardly coincides with the known facts, which are that he sailed on vessels from New Haven, traded in the West Indies, was at different times a baker, a barber, a grocer and that he pleaded the cause of Africans before the tribunal of Massachusetts. Testifying to his eloquence as a lawyer is no less a witness than Josiah Quincy, who at his last meeting with the Massachusetts Historical Society said he remembered Peters well and had often met him in the courtroom.

(NOTE: See Records of the Massachusetts Historical Society, November 12, 1763.)

But none of these things were known to Phillis that January afternoon as they sat together in the kitchen.

"I shall be glad to call for your answer later in the week," he told her.

"You are very kind," she said and her heart was singing because he would return.

When she had closed the heavy door behind him she leaned her head against its hard surface and closed her eyes. And in that moment his face was indelibly impressed upon her heart. But when she went upstairs to ask Mary if her sick headache had gone she told her only that a messenger had brought a letter from Obour. And that evening when she was writing to her friend she added a prim postscript:

"The young man by whom this is handed you seems to me to be a very clever man and is very complaisant and agreeable."

When, several days later, the "messenger" called again and Mary met him she knew that her Phillis was in love.

As if this were not enough, two weeks later a courier brought a letter for "Miss Phillis Wheatley." Mr. Wheatley took it from him and called, "Phillis! Where are you, Phillis?"

She came running down the stairs. Any summons now might mean that *he* had come back! She took the thick letter and turned it in her hand. It was slightly soiled and the wax scarcely held.

"What is it, Phillis?" Mary appeared in the kitchen door.

"Well, open it! Open it!" Mr. Wheatley spoke impatiently since letters brought by couriers were apt to be important.

124

Her eyes went first to the bottom of the sheet and she looked up quickly.

"It's from General Washington!"

"General Washington?" Mr. Wheatley regarded the broad smiles on their faces as if he thought they were crazy. "Washington?" he asked again.

"Yes, Father." Mary tried to speak calmly. "Don't look so surprised. Remember Phillis is a poetess!"

"But what would General Washington be—?" The old gentleman's question was interrupted by Mary's urging.

"Read it, Phillis! What does he say?"

Phillis read aloud:

Cambridge, February 28th, 1776

Miss Phillis:

Your favor of the 26th of October did not reach my hands till the middle of December. Time enough, you will say to have given an answer ere this. Granted. But a variety of important occurrences continually interposing to distract the mind and withdraw the attention, I hope will apologize for the delay and plead my excuse for the seeming neglect. I thank you most sincerely for your polite notice of me in your elegant lines. However undeserving I may be of such encomium and panegyric, the style and manner exhibit a striking proof of your poetical talents. As a tribute justly due to you I would have published the poem had I not been apprehensive that while I only meant to give the world this new instance

125

of your genius, I might have incurred the imputation of vanity. This, and nothing else, determined me not to give it place in the public prints. If you should come to Cambridge or near headquarters I shall be happy to see a person so favored by the Muses, to whom Nature has been so liberal and beneficent in her dispensations. I am, with great respect, Your obedient humble servant,

George Washington

The British had drained Boston dry. They had torn up the Commons with their guns and turned Copp's Hill into a fortress; they had pulled down fences, houses and steeples, had dragged pews and altars from churches for firewood. Governor Winthrop's mansion that had stood in the heart of the town since its beginning was gone and Liberty Tree was but a stump.

But they had not subdued the people. And when early in March, 1776, Washington took possession of two large hills overlooking the southern part of Boston, the British quietly boarded their ships and, taking their Tory sympathizers with them, sailed away. The ships were not out of sight when the townspeople, anxiously waiting in Watertown, Canton, Worcester and Lexington, began streaming back. They looked about them in dismay, but soon set to work with a will cleaning away debris and re-establishing their homes.

Then on March 20th General Washington himself, at the head of his troops, marched into the town. All the bells they could salvage began to ring, and everybody stopped whatever they were doing and rushed out to meet him. They marched right down King Street. Phillis and Mary waved their kerchiefs while the children danced up and down on the walk and Mr. Wheatley stood by with his hand on his son-in-law's shoulder. Neither plumes nor gold braid flashed in the sunshine as the general came riding on his big horse—but how the people cheered!

Suddenly Phillis saw Black Prince. Head up and walking proudly he marched in the lines close behind Washington. He was looking for them and as he came opposite the house he waved.

"Look, look!" Phillis shouted. "It's Prince!"

They could do no more than call to him then, but that night he appeared. Phillis threw her arms around his neck, Mary held his hand, John Lathrop and Mr. Wheatley slapped him on his back. Everybody talked at once. Prince was somewhat overwhelmed by his welcome.

"Yo' ain't mad with me for goin' with tha soldiers?" He looked at his old master with some apprehension.

"Mad?" Mr. Wheatley's voice was gruff. "Of course not. We're proud of you!"

"I knew you hadn't joined up with the British." Phillis' eyes were shining.

Prince regarded her with astonishment. "With

127

tha British? Who? Me?" They laughed together at the joke.

But Mr. Wheatley spoke seriously. "You *are* free, Prince! If there are any papers to sign I'll see to that immediately."

They could not lay out a feast before him because they had so little food, but they heaped dried beans on his plate and told him soon the garden would be up. Prince had a few heroic exploits to relate. He had been in or around Charlestown all the time and had obeyed orders. Of course he had been somewhere on the hill last June, but during the battle, he explained, there had been so much coming and going, so much confusion, he hardly knew what he did do.

"It was awful bad!" Prince summed up the Battle of Bunker Hill briefly.

He didn't look like a hero. Before he left they went up into the garret and found some discarded clothes of Nathaniel's to replace the stained, threadbare garments he had on. Then he went back to where the soldiers were camping.

They never saw Black Prince again. When the commander-in-chief left a few days later he took the bulk of the Massachusetts troops with him to New York. Prince was in that section.

"It's too bad you didn't go to see General Washington while he was here." Mary looked up at Phillis who was bent over a tub of clothes.

Phillis twisted the garment in her hands before

answering. She had written several poems recently but no one had seen them.

"I do wish he had allowed his aide to publish the poem," she said after a moment.

There were no publishers in Boston now. Before the blockade was imposed Phillis' volume of poems had been selling at Messrs. Cox and Berry, who imported it from London. But these booksellers had not yet returned to their half-demolished shop. Phillis therefore thought wistfully of the hawk-faced Englishman who served Washington and talked of publications. If only General Washington were not so modest!

But all the gods were conspiring for Phillis' good these days. And the next morning as she walked along King Street she saw the Englishman. She smiled as he approached her.

"Welcome to our town, good sir," she said, extending her hand.

He took off his hat and bowed elegantly but she noted that his clothes were almost as threadbare and stained as were Prince's.

"Good morning, Miss Phillis," he said. "This is a good meeting because I owe you an apology."

"No need, Mr. Paine," she said. "Mr. Washington thanked me for the poem but he said why he had stopped its publication."

"I still think he's wrong. It is a good thing that all should know the high regard in which he is held by some of his countrymen. Not all his enemies are with the British."

She had heard people speak against the Virginian. Now as she heard his aide's words her face was troubled.

"Could I see his letter?" Paine asked the question abruptly.

"My house is only a few steps down the street, sir. If you will come with me?" Phillis said.

When he read the letter Paine said, "If this letter were published with the poem Washington's objections would be removed." He looked hard at Phillis. "Will you trust me with your letter?"

She did not want to let the letter out of her hands but the man's purpose was so clear and so good that she nodded her head.

"I have some interests with certain printers in Philadelphia. I'll talk to Washington again." He smiled his crooked smile and said, "We shall see."

"It seems strange that we must fight Englishmen when *he's* an Englishman," Mary said when their visitor had gone.

Phillis thought of the countess and of her friends; she thought of the fine old colonial homes and the churches that had been demolished in Boston and she spoke slowly.

"There must be a lot of different kinds of people in the world. And I don't think fighting anybody helps to understand them."

There was hope in Boston that spring. Not only were the inhabitants rebuilding their town but they were stoutly fortifying the port against any further attack. Ships were once more going in and out of the harbor and women were once more meeting in the markets.

In May Phillis received a copy of the *Pennsylvania Magazine,* or *American Monthly Museum.* It was dated April, 1776. In it appeared her "Poem to George Washington," accompanied by the short note she had enclosed to him and the letter the general had written to her. The people of Massachusetts read the *Pennsylvania Magazine* and boasted of the poet in their midst.

On a lovely June morning Phillis looked up to see John Peters walking toward her through the garden. He smiled as he came, as though he had good news for her. He was, he announced, opening a grocery store in Court Street and would be very happy to have the patronage of the Wheatley house. Phillis replied modestly that she would speak to the master. Lingering only long enough to praise her roses the young man went away.

And on July 4th, in Philadelphia, a new nation was born.

CHAPTER ELEVEN

"I, Phillis, Take Thee, John"

From the very beginning John Peters looked upon Phillis as a "fine lady." She was a young woman with classical education—a poetess. She went everywhere in Boston, was regarded as the foster daughter of a rich merchant, traveled with his children and ate at his table. She had been abroad, lived in the home of a countess, been entertained by gentry. She had been honored with the attention of General Washington. More than anything in the world he wanted Phillis for his wife. But he was determined not to ask for her hand until he could offer her a home suitable to her "station." Such was the pride of John Peters.

But acquiring the means to procure such a home was a herculean task at a time when all the strength of the country was directed toward war and when the people were struggling to maintain mere subsistence.

There was no let up of toil and little replenishing of shortages in the Wheatley house. The men waited for some change while the women struggled to meet the daily needs. Poor Phillis knew that John loved her. As the weeks passed she ate out her heart because he did not speak.

The third year of the war was the blackest. With Washington's soldiers freezing at Valley Forge the people of Boston said they must not complain. But old men can not keep hoping when all the good they know is gone. On a blustery March morning John Wheatley did not come down to breakfast.

"Let him sleep." Mary looked at the snow beating against the window and shivered. Something like the palsy was shaking her limbs and she leaned over the stove where green wood smoked.

But the master did not awake. When finally Phillis tiptoed into his room she knew that he had gone to join his good wife.

After the funeral the lawyers came and Phillis sat beside Mary and her husband. For the first time it was learned that John Wheatley had been heavily in debt. For the past few years his business had been dragging him down by the force of its own weight. Nathaniel, far away in London, was somehow out of it. Much of what the lawyers said was bewildering. In closing, one of them cleared his throat and asked a question:

"The girl, Phillis—I believe she goes with the estate?"

They stared at him and Mary said rather sharply, "I don't understand."

The lawyer was apologetic. He knew enough about the Wheatleys to realize that the matter was complicated. But, he sighed, business was business.

"You realize, Mrs. Lathrop, that your father's estate will have to be settled so you can claim your inheritance. I am merely trying to itemize the estate."

"But you said—you asked—?" Mary stopped. Sudden understanding made her turn pale.

"All pieces of your father's property must be included," explained the lawyer.

Phillis turned to ice. Somewhere mixed with the pounding in her ears sounded the word *slave*. Then Mary was gripping her hand and saying,

"Phillis is a *free* woman!"

"Oh," said the lawyer, "she has the papers?"

"You doubt my word?" Mary's voice was icy. "I was witness to the manumission."

When the lawyers had gone they sat together in dazed despondency. The house would be sold. Mary and Phillis looked around the room at all the familiar objects that had spelled "home" for as long as they could remember. Reverend Lathrop would of course provide a home for his family, but Mary knew very well how uncertain his support from the church was. The thought that this house built by her father, where she and her brother had been born, should go to strangers was intolerable.

"I'll write Nat," she said a little wildly. "He'll save the house."

"It will be six months before you can hear from Nathaniel," responded her husband. "And even the house will not settle everything."

Phillis said nothing. And that silence said more than many words. What was she to do? Where would she go? Fear clutched at her heart.

"Miss Mary," her low voice trembled, "are there any papers—about me?"

Mary Lathrop tried to speak. Her eyes filled with tears and she began to cry. Her husband put his arm about her.

"Don't, my dear, you'll be sick." He shook his head at Phillis.

Phillis turned and went up to her room. For the first time since they had brought her to the house she seemed to hear the clank of chains about her ankles. Phillis knew that Mary was afraid—afraid for her. Afraid lest Phillis might be claimed as a slave—a piece of property to settle John Wheatley's debts.

The dark girl fell upon her knees, her face against the bed. And gradually the turmoil subsided. She looked back to a lovely June morning—to a morning when she first opened her eyes and saw the garden—and how out of the green had come voices and soft loving hands: Mrs. Wheatley,

Aunt Sukey, Mary with her golden hair in her eyes and Nat who laughed and gave her apples. And as the memories pressed in, her heart began to sing, words formed on her lips:

> 'Twas mercy brought me from my pagan land,
> Taught my benighted soul to understand
> That there's a God, that there's a Saviour too;
> Who died for me through love I never knew.

Phillis lifted her head and she smiled. The singing in her heart swelled to a chorus:

> Arise, my soul, on wings enraptured, rise
> To praise the monarch of the earth and skies,
> Whose goodness and beneficence appear
> As round its center moves the rolling year.

She bowed her head again—this time in gratitude. She had so much—so much of love. For John was close by! He would know that she needed him now. He would help them now.

Phillis got up hastily. She must go down. She must tell Mary not to be afraid. Once more she squared her shoulders and out of the depth of her love and faith poured strength.

The news that the Wheatleys had lost their home shook John Peters. He knew that war was bringing ruin to many houses. But he had looked upon John Wheatley as a retired merchant of considerable means. The knowledge that Mr. Wheatley had died

deeply in debt that the family home had been
ken away meant real privation.

Peters' own fortunes were precarious to say the
ast. Court Street had not turned out to be a good
cation for his grocery store and he had recently
oved into Queen. There he hoped to do better.
e slept on a cot in the shop and he was turning
ck every shilling for goods. Everything imported
as exceedingly high and the farmers scarcely
othered to bring in meat. Peters went over these
nsiderations carefully.

And yet—when he took Phillis' two small hands
his and asked, "What are you going to do?" she
ised her dark eyes to his and said, "I don't
ow."

And he, being a man in love, swept her into his
ms and kissed her full lips.

Mary was delighted. This marriage, she thought,
ould solve all Phillis' problems. She was the one
o spread the news, taking care to mention casu-
y that "You know, Mother freed Phillis before
e died," or "It was so thoughtful of dear Mother
make out Phillis' free papers before she died."

Mr. Wimby of Wimby, Wimby and Squires,
torneys, was for going further into this mat-
.

"*I* should like to see those papers," he remarked
idly.

But his partners reasoned with him.

"John Wheatley and his father before him were
e men. It is not fitting that we subject his

daughter to questions which may be—er—shall we
say embarrassing. Besides, we must remember that
the girl, Phillis, is held in high regard."

So the question was allowed to rest. Indeed, few
of the townspeople noted the breaking up of the
Wheatley home. Most of the old friends had either
died or gone away. Those who remained, managed
in half-demolished houses or were crowded in with
younger relatives. The good days of neighborly
gossip, of leisurely visits across yards and of after-
noons sewing together under the trees were no
more. The war had turned Boston into a bleak
town of hard-faced, hurrying men and aging wom-
en in dusty black.

All too quickly the time came when they must
prepare to leave the house. Papers had been signed
and creditors were waiting to take over.

"Lie quiet, Miss Mary. You look peaked. I'll
pack these." Phillis gently pushed her toward the
couch. Warm sunshine streamed through the open
windows and the little girl's laughter floated in
from the garden. Mary sank back gratefully. The
pain in her side was bringing little beads of perspi-
ration to her brow but she held back the moan that
rose behind clenched teeth. Phillis must have her
happiness!

They were stripping the house. Rugs, drapes
and furniture would have to be left but creditors
were allowing them to take all personal belong-

gs. So they carried down trunks from the attic,
ok pictures from the walls and emptied chests.

"You must have china and linen," Mary said
ying aside a lovely damask cloth.

And tears filled Phillis' eyes as she folded the
esses her dear mistress had worn. Yet there was
pain in the tears for everything they touched
ought tender memories. It was those memories
ey were packing now—memories to take with
em.

There could be no doubt of the singing in
illis' heart. As Mary watched the dark face she
ed to put aside her disappointment and anxieties
d envision a bright future for her children. Sure-
the war would end this summer. They would
ild a new house then. Soon her little son would
learning his A B C's. She must not worry. But
could not put away the gnawing pain in her
e.

John Peters came often now. He helped with the
cking, relieved them of errands. The Reverend
throp regarded him with some skepticism.

"He's too good looking!" John Lathrop told his
fe.

The garden bloomed its fairest that June. Mis-
ss Wheatley's hyacinths seemed bent on filling
place and every blossom knew it had a special
ssion to perform. For here under the trellis of
roses Phillis was married.

The birds in the trees furnished music and gold-
butterflies were the decoration. Mary had in-

sisted that Phillis put on a cream-colored silk dre
she had worn once in England. When the slend
bride walked across the green grass toward hi
John Peters' eyes lighted with pride. He had b
"fine lady."

It was their last day in the old house and it w
right that the day should be happy. After the bri
ceremony they drank a toast in fine wine. The
John Peters lifted his wife into the smart lit
chaise he had procured for the day and they dro
away.

Phillis looked back for what she knew would
her last look at Mary standing in the doorwa
And the sunlight falling on her transformed t
faded locks into gold once more. Her eyes smile
satisfied. As the dark woman turned and slipp
her hand into her husband's, she heard across t
years that voice assuring a frightened child:

"Your name is Phillis."

CHAPTER TWELVE

'Tis Freedom's Sacrifice

Lo freedom comes. The prescient muse foretold,
All eyes th'accomplished prophecy behold;
She, the bright progeny of Heaven, descends,
And every grace her sovereign step attends.
Fixed is our new-born nation's lustrous line,
And bids in thee her future council shine;
To every realm her portals opened wide
Receives from each the full commercial tide;
Each art and science now with rising charms
She welcomes gladly with expanded arms.

There is a singing that does not die. Such singing was in Phillis Wheatley's heart. The war dragged on and everywhere want stalked through the land.

Even the bright beginning of her marriage was dimmed by Mary's illness. For when, all beaming with happiness, she hastened for the first visit in the little house off North Square she found Mary very sick. That night when John hurried home to his bride he found her face clouded with worry.

"I must help her, John. Dear John, I have to stay with her now." Phillis searched her husband's face for understanding.

Certainly this was not what John wanted. He knew Phillis was not strong. He wanted to take care of her. But he knew the heart of Phillis. And so he did not hold her.

Mary Wheatley Lathrop died August 24, 1778.

The children clung weeping to Phillis' skirts and after the funeral was over Phillis wanted to take them home with her.

"I'll keep them, Reverend Lathrop," she said, "until you can make plans."

The stricken man regarded her dully. He knew that she and John Peters were living in the back room of the store. He knew that Peters had little business. Phillis seemed to read his thoughts.

"John may have found a house by now, sir," she added brightly. "I'll take good care of the children."

The Reverend Lathrop shook his head and said, "Your heart is the best, Phillis. God keep you well!" He sighed brokenly. "We'll move in with one of the members of the church."

Phillis left the house clean and neat and the children quietly playing in the back yard. She slipped out, taking care that they did not see her go. Her heart ached for them. Heat curled and quivered in the still glare of the sun as she made her way toward Queen Street. As she went along fatigue slipped away and sorrow was replaced by the thought of John. It had been days since she had seen him.

As Phillis neared her section of the town the streets became narrower and shade trees disappeared. But before the war Queen had been a busy street of small shops. As she turned the corner into Queen Phillis saw that workmen had started pulling down the partially burned buildings on the corner lot. The air was filled with dust and as she hurried by she began to cough. The store was in the middle of the block and she half expected to see John on the sidewalk changing a sign or arranging products for display. She was still smiling with anticipation when she saw the wooden boards nailed across the door. The store was boarded up!

With her heart in her mouth Phillis made her way through the alley to the back. The back door stood open to the hot glare of the sun. She found John sitting on an empty cask in the bare room. He sat there holding his head in his hands and did not hear her until she called softly.

"John!"

For a moment his eyes flooded with joy. Then she saw the light blot out and he groaned.

"What is it, John?" she asked. "What has happened?"

He seemed to sink into himself, his eyes fixed on the floor.

"The store—it's—" he began. After a moment he continued, "They're clearing out all this block. I had to let the store go."

"You *sold* out?" Phillis asked.

John had difficulty with his answer. When it came it was a husky whisper. "They took it—for debts."

The full weight of his words was like a blow. But before she could speak he had taken her in his arms, his lips against her cheek.

"Don't, Phillis! Don't cry! I'll take care of you. We'll go to the country. That's what you need. I'll work through the harvest. See, Phillis, I have packed your things. They are all here. Nothing has been taken."

He pointed to a large box against the wall. After a time Phillis lifted the cover. There lay the gleaming damask cloth, the lovely dress, the small pieces of fine lace and the big knitted shawl of many colors. Susannah Wheatley had made the shawl with her own hands. This box held the portion which Mary had said was hers—hers to take to the new home. Phillis choked back her tears.

The box went with them on the cart when they

144

drove out to the country the next morning. John's plan was to drive through the farm lands and offer himself as an "extry" during the busy season of fruit picking and harvesting. He had rented the high cart with great wooden wheels and the old nag with the promise that he would pay when he returned.

They went from place to place, all the time going farther toward the Berkshire Hills. Sometimes they slept in the cart, sometimes on the ground, sometimes in a shed. As long as the weather was good this gypsylike life was not unpleasant. They might have enjoyed it thoroughly had it not been for the fact that work was so scarce. Farmers had not bothered to plant much that year. Prices were so poor that they did not care whether or not the fruit was picked; they let crops rot in the fields.

They stayed in the Berkshire Valley that winter where John worked on a dairy farm. And in the spring little Johnny was born.

Phillis held her son close to her heart and marveled at their good fortune. The room over the barn was warm and dry. The farmer and his wife had been generous and good. Everything would be all right now. She wrapped her baby in the warm shawl of many colors.

Late that summer they returned to Boston and John Peters secured work on a vessel which ran up and down the Atlantic seaboard, stopping at all the ports. Merchants were trying desperately to rebuild commerce which had been destroyed by the war.

In October Phillis wrote,

Dear Obour:

By this opportunity I have the pleasure to inform you that I am well and hope you are so. Though I have been silent I have not been unmindful of you, but a variety of hindrances was the cause of my not writing. But in time to come I hope our correspondence will revive—and revive for better times. Pray write me soon, for I long to hear from you. You may depend on constant replies. I wish you much happiness, and am, dear Obour, your friend and sister, Phillis Peters.

John was away now for days at a time. Ship work was hazardous so that every hour until he returned was anxious for Phillis. She did what she could to turn the two-room shack into a home. Always in the way was the big box. How could she use the linen—the damask cloth, the dress or the pieces of lace? One day as she was rocking the baby to sleep a thought occurred to her. She used only one small stick of wood at a time because the pile was low and she needed her store of change for food. But while the baby slept she opened the box, took out the fine laces and, slipping them inside her dress, went out. She was gone only a short time. When she returned she came carrying a fresh load of wood. Later she went out with her pail for milk. For several days she and the baby ate well and the room was warm.

She was working on a proposal for publishing another volume of poems. A second edition of her first poems had finally been brought out in Boston, but the bookshop burned shortly afterward and few copies had been sold.

On October 30th, 1779, a proposal appeared in the *Evening Post and General Advertiser*: "For printing by subscriptions a volume of Poems and Letters on various subjects, dedicated to the Right Hon. Benjamin Franklin, Esq. one of the Ambassadors of the United States at the Court of France"—By Phillis Peters.

In the list of poems offered are "Thoughts on the Times," "On the Capture of General Charles Lee," "On the Death of General Wooster," "To his Excellency General Washington," "Farewell to England" and "Niagara." Among the letters is one "To Dr. Benjamin Rush of Philadelphia."

Of this collection *The Evening Post* says,

The subjects are various and curious, and the author, a Female African, whose lot it was to fall into the hands of a generous master and great benefactor. The learned and ingenious, as well as those who are pleased with novelty, are invited to incourage the publication—the former that they may fan the sacred fire which is self-enkindled in the breast of this Young African:—The ingenuous that they may in reading this collection have a large play for their imaginations, and be excited to please and benefit mankind by some brilliant production of their own pens:—Those who are always in search of some new thing, that they may obtain a sight of this *Rara Avis in Terra*:—And every one that the ingenious may be encouraged to improve her own mind and benefit and please mankind.

The work was to be printed on good paper, set in neat type and would contain about three hundred pages in octavo.

Months passed and the work was not printed. When in October, 1781, word came that Cornwallis had surrendered at Yorktown, Phillis wrote:

> Hail, happy day, when, smiling like the morn,
> Fair Freedom rose New England to adorn;
> Elate with hope her race no longer mourns,
> Each soul expands, each grateful bosom burns.
> No more America in mournful strain
> Of wrongs, and grievance unredressed complain,
> No longer shalt thou dread the iron chain
> Which wanton Tyranny with lawless hand
> Made, and intended to enslave the land.

At last all would be well. John Peters lifted his small son in his arms and said, "Now you'll get fat, little man!" And he hurried out, intent on a bright, new project.

Phillis held the child close to her bosom for a few minutes. He had been too small since the day of his birth. He needed lots of milk. Perhaps now she would be able to get fresh milk. She looked down into her son's golden face so like his father's and she marveled anew at the soft, black hair on his head and big eyes. The baby smiled.

"You are so beautiful," she said. "And you are mine!"

She added several new poems to the manuscript that month.

"They'll be printed soon!" she was assured.

Altogether those poems gave a colorful account of the struggle out of which the nation had been born. She waited impatiently for their appearance.

But the volume did not come out. Boston had been sacrificed in the struggle for freedom. Her population had been scattered, her trade ruined. For a hundred years her wealth had come largely from commerce with the West Indies. These islands were closed to her now by England. The soldiers returning to former pursuits found no place for themselves. They wandered about, sick, idle, hungry, sometimes desperate. People were bewildered to find that peace and plenty had not come back hand in hand.

In the spring of 1783 hope poured through Phillis' veins like wine. Nathaniel was coming home! A letter written six months before finally reached her—a letter which said:

Dear Phillis,
   Though it might seem near all I hold dear in

America has been swept away I am coming home. My wife fears the rigors of the voyage but I shall come though only for a short stay. I would visit the graves of my father and mother and my dear sister. I would see you once again, dear Phillis, for you are all that is left of our home. In her last letter Mary told me of your happy marriage. I broke off writing to America when Mary died so I have never wished you joy. But I shall mend that lack. The news we have from Boston is bad. I hope you and your husband are in good health and that all goes well with you. Soon I shall see you in your home and if things are not as I hope perhaps I can lend a hand. Until then, Phillis, I am, your sincere and faithful friend,

Nathaniel Wheatley

Poor Nat! Phillis' first emotion was one of warm sympathy. She sensed his loneliness and heart-break. Then she looked around the bare room. "Soon I shall see you in your home," he had written. The joy she felt on opening his letter receded a little.

Their "home" was one of the miserable back-lot houses stuck in behind better and more elegant houses facing the street. Boston was honeycombed with narrow, crooked alleys which served these tiny houses crowded together on back lots. She knew how John hated the place and he had sworn he would get her and the children out before hot weather set in. The little boy was three now and had a two-month-old baby sister called Susie.

Phillis roused herself and looked once more at the date on the letter. It was October 25, 1782. It was now May 1st. That meant that Nathaniel may have already reached Boston. He might be coming any minute! She sprang up and went about setting her house in order. She swept and cleaned and washed and polished the two rooms; she bathed the alley grime from her son's body. Clothed in his "best suit" and instructed to "Sit quiet!" he regarded her solemnly.

When John came home he took no notice of anything until she told him. Then his face darkened and he spoke harshly:

"I don't want him here!"

Phillis said nothing for a moment. She understood why John spoke as he did. She knew how he suffered because of the things he could not do. She knew that life was hurting him. She loved him and she understood.

"John," she asked gently, "would you have me turn one who is like my brother from our door? Read his letter!" And she handed it to him.

She saw his face break while he read. Then he put his head down on the table and a sob tore from his throat.

"This hovel! This hole!" he gasped.

She put her arms about his neck and she laid her cheek close against his.

"I love you, John," she whispered. "I love you."

After that it was easier to say "We'll talk things

over when he comes." And John Peters kept on trying. Perhaps all men's hands were not against him. Surely there was something a capable man of some attainments could find to do—even though he were a Negro. But the jobs were few and far between.

Phillis finally began inquiring about Nathaniel from persons she knew he would contact. He did not come nor did anyone hear from him. The weeks of waiting lengthened into months.

People who lived in the alley did not know that their children were taking sick because of the green scum on the alley well. And as the heat became more intense flies swarmed everywhere.

One day Phillis looked up from the tub of clothes she was washing to see small Johnny standing in the doorway, both dirty hands over his stomach, his little face puckered as if in pain.

"Did you fall, honey?" asked the mother wiping suds from her hands and starting toward him. But with a whimper of pain the child dropped in a heap at her feet.

Phillis laid him on the cot, bathed his face, rubbed his hands in hers. But the big eyes stared at her blankly.

"Johnny! Johnny!" The quivering inside her shook her voice and made her hands tremble. "Oh, God, help me!" she prayed. Steadied a little she rushed out to find a doctor.

That good man came as soon as he could. He knew it was a futile trip. The next day Johnny died. And the singing heart of Phillis was dumb with pain.

It was the father who thought of Nathaniel's letter—of his promises to Phillis.

"Why did he lie? Why did he pretend to care what becomes of us?" John Peters looked at the still face of his wife and bitterness replaced despair in his heart. Years later he learned that the reason Nathaniel Wheatley did not come to them that summer of 1783 was that he had passed away in London.

But now John Peters grew reckless.

"I'll try anything!" he said.

He was not a knave or a thief. In the 1790's when Boston had managed to steady itself and some degree of business and commerce had revived, we find John Peters practicing law in the courts. They say that then his face was cold and hard—that he tracked down his opponent without leniency: he made money. But there was nothing in his heart, for he felt he had lost Phillis and everything that he held dear.

In the fall of 1784 John Peters was thrown into debtors' prison. This was a custom of the times. More than one Revolutionary officer was in jail for debt. But this deprived Phillis and the baby even of precarious and uncertain support.

Phillis was taken on as a scrub woman in one of the new boarding houses. She got her food and a few pennies to take home. The work was hard and

153

at night when she hurried home to the baby her body ached with pain.

The bitter cold of winter closed in on Boston early that year. With each day the problem of keeping the child warm became more acute. She had sold everything from the box except the shawl. One night when she was torn between the need for fuel or food for the baby she wrapped the shawl about her shoulders and went to the shop. Perhaps the man would let her have a little wood on credit.

"I'll bring you the money tomorrow," she said. "Tonight I have only enough pennies for bread and milk. If you would—let me have—just—a little wood."

"Wood's high," observed the shopkeeper.

"That's a right pretty shawl you got there," the shopkeeper's wife called out from her corner.

Phillis clutched the warm folds. The shawl! Perhaps—but she shivered. Then she saw the baby again—alone—in the freezing room.

"If you'd let me have the wood," she said timidly, "I could leave the shawl—for guarantee."

"She talks fine!" observed the shopkeeper to his wife.

"Wanna sell the shawl?" asked the woman bluntly.

In the end she let it go.

The people at the boardinghouse complained about her coughing. After a time it was better

ie still and hold her baby close. She could not go
ut. The wood was used up.

"If only John were here! But he's in prison!"
There was no one.

She did not feel the cold on that December 5th,
784, for she was listening to the singing of the
niverse. She had heard it in the flowers of the
arden, she had greeted the sun as it came up over
ie treetops and she had greeted a nation as it rose
om the ashes of great sacrifice. She had already
ritten her own best epitaph:

> But when these shades of time are chased away,
> And darkness ends in everlasting day,
> On what seraphic pinions shall we move,
> And view the landscapes in the realms above?
> There shall my tongue in heav'nly murmurs flow,
> And there my muse with heav'nly transport glow;
> No more to tell of Damon's tender sighs,
> Or rising radiance of Aurora's eyes,
> For nobler themes demand a nobler strain,
> And purer language on th'ethereal plane.
> Cease, gentle muse! the solemn gloom of night
> Now seals the fair creation from my sight.

illis Wheatley was dead!

LIBERTY AND PEACE

This poem was published in Boston in 1784, a few
days after Phillis Wheatley's death.

Lo freedom comes. Th' prescient muse foretold,
All eyes th'accomplished prophecy behold:
Her port described, "She moves divinely fair,
Olive and laurel bind her golden hair."
She, the bright progeny of Heaven, descends,
And every grace her sovereign step attends;
For now kind Heaven, indulgent to our prayer,
In smiling peace resolves the din of war.
Fixed in Columbia her illustrious line,[1]
And bids in thee her future council shine.
To every realm her portals opened wide,
Receives from each the full commercial tide.
Each art and science now with rising charms,
She welcomes gladly with expanded arms.
E'en great Britannia sees with dread surprise,
And from the dazzling splendors turns her eyes.
Britain, whose navies swept th' Atlantic o'er,
And thunder sent to every distant shore;
E'en thou, in manners cruel as thou art,
The sword resigned, resume the friendly part.
For Gallia's power espoused Columbia's cause,[2]

---

[1] In the 18th century this continent was more often called
Columbia than America. This poem was written before the
United States as a single nation was constituted.

[2] "Gallia" refers to France.

And new-born Rome shall give Britannia laws.
Nor unremembered in the grateful strain,
Shall princely Louis' friendly deeds remain;
The generous prince impending vengeance eyes,
Sees the fierce wrong and to the rescue flies.
Perish that thirst of boundless power, that drew
On Albion's head the curse to tyrants due.
But thou appeased submit to Heaven's decree,
That bids this realm of freedom rival thee.
Now sheathe the sword that bade the brave atone
With guiltless blood for madness not their own.
Sent from enjoyment of their native shore,
Ill-fated—never to behold her more.
From every kingdom there on Europe's coast
Thronged many troops, their glory, strength, and
    boast.[3]
With heart-felt pity fair Hibernia saw
Columbia menaced by the Tyrant's law:
On hostile fields fraternal arms engage,
And mutual death, all dealt with mutual rage.
The muse's ear hears mother Earth deplore
Her ample surface smoke with kindred gore;
The hostile field destroys the social ties,
And everlasting slumber seals their eyes.
Columbia mourns, the haughty foes deride,
Her treasures plundered and her towns destroyed.
Witness how Charlestown's curling smokes arise,
In sable columns to the clouded skies.[4]
The ample dome, high-wrought with curious toil,

---

[3] Great Britain hired troops from the continent and sent them
against the American colonies.

"Hibernia" is Ireland.

[4] Reference to the Battle of Bunker Hill.

In one sad hour the savage troops despoil.
Descending peace the power of war confounds,
From every tongue celestial peace resounds:
As from the east the mighty king of day,
With rising radiance dirves the shades away,
So freedom comes arrayed with charms divine,
And in her train commerce and plenty shine.

Britannia owns her independent reign,
Hibernia, Scotia and the realms of Spain;
And great Germania's ample coast admires
The generous spirit that Columbia fires.
Auspicious Heaven shall fill with favoring gales,
Where e'er Columbia spreads her swelling sails:
To every realm shall peace her charms display,
And heavenly freedom spread her golden ray.

SOURCES

There are many sources for material on the life of Phillis Wheatley. I list here the more important original ones.

1773 *Poems on Various Subjects,* by Phillis Wheatley, Printed for A. Bell, Bookseller, London.
With Affidavit signed by Boston citizens and Letter by John Wheatley. This first edition may now be found only in collections of rare books, but it has been reprinted, with a long essay by Herbert Renfro under the title "The Life and Works of Phillis Wheatley," published in Washington, 1916.

1774 Notice in the *Boston Gazette,* January 24th:
"This day published, adorned with an Elegant Engraving of the Author, Poems on Various Subjects—by Phillis Wheatley. Sold by Messrs. Cox & Berry at their store in King Street, Boston.

1776 *Pennsylvania Magazine or American Monthly Museum* for April.

1779 Boston *Evening Post and General Advertiser,* October 30th.

1784 Boston *Independent Chronicle,* December 8, 1784:
"Last Lord's day, died Mrs. Phillis Peters (formerly Phillis Wheatley) aged 31, known to the

literary world by her celebrated Miscellaneous Poems. . . ."

1785   "Essay on the Slavery and Commerce of the Human Species," by Thomas Clarkson. This Latin dissertation won the first prize in the University of Cambridge in the year 1785.

1793   *Poems of Phillis Wheatley,* published by Barber & Southwick, Albany.

De la Littérature des Nègres, by Abbé Gregoire, Paris, 1808.

Memoir of Phillis by Margaretta M. Odell, Published by George W. Light, Boston, 1834

Records of the Massachusetts Historical Society, 1863–1864.

Index

INDEX